Brahms' Symphonies

A CLOSER LOOK

MAGNUM OPUS

Edited by Robert Levine

Magnum Opus is a series for anyone seeking a greater familiarity with the cornerstones of Western Classical Music—operatic, choral, and symphonic. An erudite collection of passionate, down-to-earth, and authoritative books on the works and their creators, Magnum Opus will build into an indispensable resource for anyone's musical library.

Forthcoming:

Beethoven's Fifth and Seventh Symphonies, by David Hurwitz

Handel's Messiah, by Ben Finane

Brahms' Symphonies

A CLOSER LOOK

David Hurwitz

continuum

NEW YORK • LONDON

2009

The Continuum International Publishing Group Inc
80 Maiden Lane, New York, NY 10038

The Continuum International Publishing Group Ltd
The Tower Building, 11 York Road, London SE1 7NX
www.continuumbooks.com

Library of Congress Cataloging-in-Publication Data
Hurwitz, David, 1961–
  Brahms's symphonies : a closer look / by David Hurwitz.
     p. cm.—(Magnum opus)
  Includes bibliographical references.
  ISBN-13: 978-0-8264-3164-6 (pbk. : alk. paper)
  ISBN-10: 0-8264-3164-X (pbk. : alk. paper) 1. Brahms, Johannes,
1833–1897. Symphonies. 2. Symphonies—Analysis, appreciation.
I. Title. II. Series.
  ML410.B8H73 2009
  784.2'184092—dc22
                                                              2009010232

Printed in the United States of America

To Bob:
Brahms once referred to Dvořák as a "real Mensch."
I couldn't have said it better.

Contents

1 INTRODUCTION: BRAHMS' HISTORICAL
  FOOT PROBLEM   1

2 THE ROAD TO THE SYMPHONIES:
  BRAHMS VERSUS THE ORCHESTRA   23

3 SYMPHONY NO. 1 IN C MINOR, OP. 68 (1876)   35

4 SYMPHONY NO. 2 IN D MAJOR, OP. 73 (1877)   72

5 SYMPHONY NO. 3 IN F MAJOR, OP. 90 (1883)   96

6 SYMPHONY NO. 4 IN E MINOR, OP. 98 (1885)   121

  DISCOGRAPHY OF RECOMMENDED
  RECORDINGS   145

  ANNOTATED BIBLIOGRAPHY   149

Chapter 1

Introduction: Brahms' Historical Foot Problem

IF THE LEGACY of Brahms' music proves anything, it is that in art, as in any other commodity, there's value in scarcity. His modern reputation rests on a small handful of chamber works, a few songs, *A German Requiem*, and exactly thirteen orchestral works: four symphonies, four concertos, two overtures, two serenades, and one set of variations. Despite his legendary fastidiousness and painstakingly high level of craftsmanship, his output, like that of most composers active in a wide range of media, varies both in quality and popularity. Thus, out of approximately two hundred songs, only a tiny handful is well-known today. A vast quantity of choral music sits on library shelves, including *Rinaldo*, his second-largest (and certainly dullest) work for voices and orchestra. His chamber music for strings without piano, including the three quartets, tends to garner respect more than active enthusiasm. Even among those thirteen orchestral works, the two early serenades are easier to find on recordings than in concert.

This is not the place to question the judgment of history. What matters for our purposes is that the winnowing process that the term "judgment of history" suggests really did happen, indeed is still ongoing. It's what has created the canon of great works that fall under the general rubric of "classical music." Perhaps no composer in our Western tradition was more acutely aware of this fact, indeed obsessed and tormented by it, than was Brahms. His comment about being intimidated by the "tramping steps of a giant" (i.e., Beethoven) behind him when writing a symphony is deservedly famous. But the problem went deeper than that. "This much I do know," Brahms wrote to Clara Schumann using yet another foot analogy, "in everything...that I attempt, I step on the heels of forerunners who make me feel self-conscious."

Many great composers kept at least one eye on posterity if they lived to an age where they could imagine their lives drawing to a natural close. Bach's magnificent works of summation, such as the Mass in B Minor and The Art of Fugue, reflect this awareness. So do Haydn's late Masses and oratorios, or Beethoven's last piano sonatas and string quartets. Brahms is different. He lived at the beginning of the age when the best works of the past were being sifted, catalogued, printed, revived, and ultimately enshrined in the pantheon of classics that we still acknowledge today. Henceforth, modern music would have to fight for its place in the affections of listeners against the growing body of accepted masterpieces by dead composers. Despite this daunting prospect, at a very early stage in his career Brahms decided that he would only write music that he deemed worthy of comparison to this imposing historical legacy.

The quality that Brahms valued above all others was the highest possible level of compositional craftsmanship. It could hardly be otherwise given the context in which he wanted his work to be heard and understood. Brahms framed it this way in a conversation with his friend, noted baritone and (later) conductor George Henschel: "One ought never to forget that by actually perfecting *one* piece one gains and learns more than by commencing or half-finishing a dozen. Let it rest, let it rest, and keep going back to it and working at it over and over again, until it is completed as a finished work of art, until there is not a note too much or too little, not a bar you could improve upon. Whether it is *beautiful* also, is an entirely different matter, but perfect it *must* be. You see, I am rather lazy, but I never cool down over a work, once begun, until it is perfected, unassailable."

This is the philosophy that allowed Brahms to spend years, even decades, tinkering with a single piece before allowing it to see the light of day. It also accounts for the apparent lack of stylistic progress from early works to late (though inevitably there was some), as well as his much-vaunted conservatism and his disdain for contemporary notions of musical progress. For how else could he define "perfection" other than in terms of what the classical masters of the past, both immediate and more distant, achieved? This emphasis on exalted standards of craftsmanship, on polish and formal shapeliness, naturally has consequences in terms of emotional expression, particularly to the extent that other composers have demonstrated a more impressive ability to project a wide range of feeling, or give their music a more potent sense of spontaneity and freshness.

In other words, the effort that Brahms put into his music sometimes shows, and to be honest, not always in a good way. He seemed willing to accept the limitations and trade-offs that his approach imposed; but we must take care to define these limitations accurately. They are often misunderstood or exaggerated, not least thanks to some of the clues left behind by Brahms himself. "Passions are not an inherent attribute of mankind," he insisted. "They are always exceptions or excesses. The person in whom they exceed normal bounds must consider himself an invalid, and must take care of his life and his health with medicine. Calm in joy and calm in pain and sorrow is the beautiful, true human being. Passions must soon fade away, or they must be driven off."

Brahms said it, but did he really believe it in life as in music, or was he just doing his best to offer helpful advice in his letter to the long-suffering and frequently depressed Clara Schumann? The music very often suggests otherwise despite (or even because of) the fierce discipline of its writing. We must take great care not to let the evidence of our eyes, and in particular that of words uttered privately and without specific reference to music, override the proof that reaches our ears. Brahms' philosophy of life and art lives in the body of work that he left us. Rummaging through the dusty attic of his fragmentary written or reported statements as often as not breeds confusion.

I begin this discussion in confronting these issues head-on because Brahms was without question one of the most inscrutable characters in all of nineteenth-century music. His obsession with his place in history led him to take heroic measures to safeguard his privacy and his reputation. He destroyed his sketches and dozens of unpublished works, burned as many of his letters as he could retrieve, and was every bit as concerned (if in a different way) as the pamphleteering Wagner in creating and controlling his public persona. Because Brahms throughout his life played his emotional cards so close to his vest, nothing that he said can be taken without a large grain of salt as evidence of his true feelings.

However, and despite the inclinations cited thus far, Brahms did not become a colossal bore, concealing his inhibitions behind a superior technique and an elitist exploitation of current notions of respectability and "good taste." Even as a painter can illustrate the same scene using a variety of different media, from oils, to pastels, to charcoal sketches, so too a composer may explore many paths, each with its own perfectly valid and convincing final result, and each beautiful in a strongly characteristic way. Ultimately, if Brahms didn't deliver the emotional goods, I would not be writing this book and you would not be reading it.

Two factors—one a mystery, the other a conviction— saved him from terminal dullness and mediocrity, and with them the historical oblivion that he so feared. The mystery lies in the fact that he was a genius, a quality as inexplicable as it is indisputable. The conviction can be found in a letter Brahms wrote to Clara Schumann in 1858. "Art is a republic," he told her. "You should accept this principle much more wholeheartedly than you do.... Do not confer a higher rank upon any artist, and do not expect the minor ones to look up to him as something higher, as consul. His ability will make him a beloved and respected citizen of this republic, but no consul or emperor."

In other words, to be an artist is not to stand above society, to preach to the masses, or to seek to be placed on a pedestal. Brahms wrote for the normal, music-loving people of his day. He cared deeply that his music should be understood, enjoyed, even loved. His need for public acceptance coupled with his refusal to compromise his standards and "write down" to his audience naturally forced him to walk a very fine line between musical sophistication for its own sake and easy accessibility. Few composers have proven to be more successful at this particular high-wire act. Brahms was one of the very few men in history who ultimately made a living, and a good one, from composing more than from performing. At his best he challenges his listeners, but he also rewards them generously for their efforts.

If Brahms' views on the expression of passion contradicted the prevailing "let it all hang out" Romantic aesthetic of his day, then his egalitarian sentiments were even more reactionary at a time when artists viewed themselves (and were often viewed) as the high priests of national culture, the keepers of a sacred flame. Brahms himself came to be seen this way, and accepted it after his own grumpy fashion—in the event he really had little choice about what others thought and felt about the matter. But despite all of the adulation and hero worship that came to him later in life, he remained determinedly the proud product of his respectable, lower-middle-class Hamburg childhood.

As a person, Brahms was famously surly, even obnoxious, as often to his friends as to strangers, and for all the liberal sentiments just expressed almost frighteningly single-minded and egotistical. In other words, he was very much a self-absorbed artist. Although an ardent patriot in a time of passionate, often violent nationalism (one of his great heroes was Bismarck, the architect of German unification), he was no bigot by contemporary standards. For example, many of his closest friends and supporters were Jewish, and at a time when Viennese politics was turning viciously racist, he reportedly exclaimed emphatically: "Anti-Semitism is madness!"

Perhaps his single most redeeming character trait, and it was a very large one, was his unfailing generosity with money to friends and family. Indeed, it probably wouldn't be going too far to say that he used money as a sort of surrogate for the kind of emotional support he was either unwilling or unable to provide. He believed that in order to create musical works that stood worthy of a permanent place in history, he would either have to subordinate all deep human attachments to that one goal, or forgo them entirely. Financial generosity permitted the expression of affection in a material way, free of debilitating and time-consuming emotional entanglements.

This last point then raises an obvious question. What exactly is the nature of Brahmsian emotion? Does his music invite us to share in his deepest feelings, in true Romantic fashion, or is he cleverly manipulating ours? You might, with good reason, find the very dichotomy a false one. Music is as it sounds to each person. Issues such as emotional sincerity or the sources of expression may be debated, but can never be proven in any meaningful way. And yet, these questions are relevant for the light that they shed on yet another issue, perhaps *the* defining aesthetic conundrum of Brahms' life: the extent to which his music should be seen as "absolute" or "abstract," and in turn what this means for us today, as modern listeners approaching him with (hopefully) fresh ears.

The term "absolute music" turns up frequently in discussions of Brahms' art, as well as that of the classical masters: Haydn,

Mozart, and Beethoven. Its antithesis is "program music," music that tells a story or illustrates a subject, whether from literature, history, or the natural world. Both types have coexisted, side by side, since the beginning of time as far as anyone can tell. Furthermore, to the extent that all music is expressive of *something* it can be said to be programmatic. The only issue is how evident to the listener the composer intends that the *something* should be. By the same token, to the extent that any stand-alone piece of instrumental music must be formally satisfying and complete according to the purely musical criteria of theme, repetition, variation, climax, and conclusion, it can also be said to be absolute, or abstract.

In short, the distinction between the two categories is a somewhat artificial one, often a verbal convenience rather than an inherently musical fact. Beethoven summed it up nicely in describing his programmatic Pastoral Symphony (No. 6) as "More the expression of feelings than tone-painting," which is basically what all music does whether it purports to describe something concrete or not. Nevertheless, since at all periods in history music is at least as much talked about as it is listened to, this verbal distinction provides a useful and easily graspable way to define the opposing sides in what turned out to be a genuine musical war: that between the self-defined progressives led by Liszt and Wagner, who proclaimed the new era of program music, and the conservatives or "absolutists," led by Clara Schumann, violinist Joseph Joachim, and Viennese critic Eduard Hanslick, with Brahms as their figurehead.

Brahms' position in this battle was, in fact, equivocal. He both admired and claimed to understand Wagner's music better than many of his supporters, but he was very discreet about it. Joachim, on the other hand, began life as a protégé of Liszt, and later repudiated him in the nastiest possible terms. When he gave up composition to pursue his career as a traveling violin virtuoso, Brahms proved more than a match for the remaining competition (composers such as Joachim Raff, Max Bruch, Karl Goldmark, Karl Reinecke, Heinrich von Herzogenberg, Woldemar Bargiel, and numerous others). Some years previously, shortly before his untimely death in 1856, Robert Schumann had already eulogized Brahms in print as the new messiah of German music. He left his piano virtuosa wife Clara to support her large family by touring across Europe with programs often consisting primarily of music by her husband, and the young Brahms.

Meanwhile Eduard Hanslick, Vienna's most powerful critic and author of one of the most widely read (and silly, according to Brahms) aesthetic treatises *On the Beautiful in Music,* was looking for the anti-Wagner. As soon as Brahms settled permanently in Vienna in 1868 the two became close friends, bound by what could best be called opportunistic mutual affection. Although they genuinely enjoyed each other's company, Hanslick thought much of Brahms' music too cerebral and lacking in basic tunefulness, while Brahms found Hanslick's taste highly questionable. But that didn't matter. Hanslick would complain privately that a new work left him cold, and then praise it glowingly in the press. What pleased him most was that Brahms could be used as the standard by which to judge Wagner, Liszt, and their followers, and find them wanting.

Let's make one point very clear at the outset, for it will be critical to understanding Brahms' achievement as a symphonic composer. No music is written in a vacuum. Brahms' works are full of external references. He was enchanted by folk music, and particularly by Hungarian and gypsy melodies, which feature prominently not just in his famous *Hungarian Dances*, but also in the finales of his concertos and in his chamber music. The famous horn theme in the introduction to the First Symphony's finale is a genuine Swiss alphorn tune that Brahms heard while vacationing. There are also biographical allusions in the form of musical anagrams—motives and themes based on the letters or initials of friends' names.

Most of all, though, there are references to other composers' music, the pieces that Brahms loved and admired most. These can be obvious, such as the resemblance of the "big tune" in the finale of the First Symphony to the "Joy" theme in Beethoven's Ninth, or they may be concealed, private, or perhaps even unconscious tributes. One thing is certain: in seeking to place himself in the historical continuum of Western classical music, it was both inevitable and necessary that Brahms allow his listeners the opportunity to detect his awareness of, and homage to, the great works of the past. His music is not some sort of hermetically sealed oasis of abstraction and aesthetic purity, if by this we mean something that excludes all external influence.

On the other hand, such paraphrases, quotations, and other foreign bodies as Brahms does admit into the world of his instrumental works are always, as the earlier examples show, exclusively musical ones; that is, they consist largely of preexisting motives and melodies, and not mere noises that can be stylized in tones. This is particularly true of the symphonies where, for example, there are no sounds of nature, not even birdsong such as we find in Haydn, Beethoven, or Dvořák. Nor do we hear the kind of rustic dance music or folk tunes, often in the minuets and scherzos, that those composers (and many others) loved. In this respect Brahms resembles Mozart, whose entire frame of reference in his instrumental music begins and ends with human sentiment as embodied in vocal melody.

This restriction, if that's what it is, certainly proved to be no handicap to Mozart, and it wasn't one to Brahms either, at least not most of the time. The principal challenge in creating music of this type lies in the composer's ability to write affectingly: to create and develop materials that convey specific feelings in a clear and expressively convincing way. In this respect Brahms' biggest hurdle, I would suggest, was that he was almost too normal. For all that he frequently complained about loneliness, both personal and artistic, there can be no denying that he had a fantastically lucky life. Not only did he come from a good home with two loving parents who supported his musical inclinations at every turn, but he was befriended, launched on his career, and ceaselessly promoted by many of the most prominent musicians of his day.

In short, if any composer turned up in the right place at the right time, it was Brahms. Aside from his happy childhood and a personal life without the usual responsibilities of supporting a wife and family, he also enjoyed excellent health until contracting the cancer that ultimately killed him in 1897. He lived a composer's dream, able to devote himself fully to his music. To the extent that historians and music lovers equate emotional depth with biographical trauma, he should have been unspeakably shallow. He did not go insane, like Schumann; he did not die tragically young, like Mozart and Schubert (or Mendelssohn). He was not a self-aggrandizing megalomaniac, like Wagner. He did not go deaf, like Beethoven or Smetana. He was not a member of an oppressed religious or ethnic minority, like Mahler or Dvořák, nor was he a religious mystic, like Bruckner.

Naturally Brahms experienced his share of sorrow: the death of Robert Schumann, his frustrated love for Clara (and other women too), the loss of his parents; but he was anything but emotionally cold—curmudgeonly and petulant, for sure, but also extremely sensitive. Indeed, he cried at the drop of a hat. By the standards of the day his life was a breeze, and happiness ought to have been his musical specialty. How strange, then, that it wasn't. Happiness is there, certainly, but there is a great deal of moodiness, nostalgia, and above all a bittersweet lyricism that's quite special. Perhaps the most distinctive emotional quality that he captured better than almost anyone else, particularly in his orchestral works, is *rage*.

Given his remarks about the need to control passion you might find this remarkable, and so it is, but few composers wrote angrier climaxes, even whole movements, than Brahms did in his symphonies and concertos. He began his orchestral career with a particularly violent tantrum in the shape of the opening of his Piano Concerto No. 1—a colossal, fist-shaking rampage if ever there was one. You will find something similar in all of the symphonies, and we will examine each instance in its proper place in the following discussions. Where did this emotion come from? What was its source and why does it erupt so forcefully in piece after piece? The honest answer is: We don't know, but we can only be glad that it's there.

Biographers, who thrive on finding connections between an artist's life and his works, have a particularly hard time reconciling what we know about Brahms external circumstances with what we hear, and of course he did his best to make the job as difficult as possible. The most common myth you may hear told about him is that he was psychologically damaged by having to play the piano as a child of twelve in brothels and ale-houses along the Hamburg docks, where he must have both witnessed and participated in horrifying acts of sexual degradation of every kind. From these bruising experiences he emerged with a deep-seated misogyny, viewing the women he loved as pure and virginal, while seeking sexual release in the arms of prostitutes. It's a terrific story, and it does account for Brahms' perennially dysfunctional relations with the opposite sex.

Unfortunately for fans of juicy gossip, the most recent scholarship has pretty well established this view to be nonsense. Yes, Brahms probably did play the piano in local pubs of some kind to earn money for his always cash-strapped family, but they were far from the whorehouses of Brahmsian lore. More to the point, as the hugely talented, favorite child of a respectable family (his father was a well-known freelance musician and his mother a seamstress), it was hardly likely that his parents exploited his gifts with Dickensian relish by packing him off each night to some house of ill-repute. Brahms was also a sensitive child with a hyperactive imagination; he may not have *liked* his part-time job, but it hardly can have been as dire as subsequent history relates.

More significantly, there's something truly cheap in trying to tie down the epic rage that we hear in, say, the finale of the Third Symphony, to a squalid scene of child exploitation, or even worse, to the half-remembered resentments of a spoiled brat. The emotions that we hear in any piece of music, to the extent that they still move us today, have become universalized, depersonalized if you will, and while it may be nice to know where they come from and why, this information changes nothing about the impact of the work as such. I'm sure you can readily imagine one source of Brahms' rage— the attempt to ascribe particularly telling moments in a given piece to specific incidents in his life.

Brahms wanted his music to survive on its own merits, not on sensationalist propaganda or on listeners' feelings of pity for him personally. He also insisted on the composer's prerogative to write music, happy or sad, as suited him and as the materials themselves warranted. Music without words is strange among the arts in that we so often expect the work to come from the composer unbidden, the result of an inner compulsion or emotional trauma of some sort. Sometimes it does happen that way, of course, but far more often a composer decides to write a piece of music quite consciously, particularly if he is working on commission, and it's his job as a professional to be able to evoke whatever mood he chooses or the circumstances require, irrespective of extraneous considerations.

Brahms never wrote to a commission. He always had the freedom to do exactly what he wanted, but that doesn't change the basic proposition. Consider, for example, his pair of concert overtures, one called *Academic Festival* and the other *Tragic*. Brahms liked to create works in pairs, and while he designed the former as a musical "thank you" for the honorary doctorate he had received from the University of Breslau in 1879, the latter was designed simply to contrast as strongly as possible with the rowdy high spirits of the

Academic Festival. One had its origins in a real-life experience, the other in a purely musical impulse. Alternately, it would be just as fair to say that the *Tragic Overture* arose out of the same real-life experience as its companion.

Imagine how biographers would be speculating if, of the two works, only the *Tragic Overture* had survived, or even better, if Brahms had suppressed the *Academic Festival* while still in the sketch stage, burning the manuscript in one of his periodic sanitizing sprees and letting no one know that it had ever existed. It very easily could have happened that way. We would be none the wiser, and the quantity of verbal nonsense written about the surviving piece accordingly would be markedly greater. Examples such as this prove, once again, the wisdom of seeing Brahms the man as he would have preferred, through his music, rather than the other way around. In the final analysis, there is no clear biographical explanation for why Brahms sounds the way he does, and wrote the way he did.

However, if you are interested in biography and have the time and inclination to do some further reading, some fine works are readily available. Jan Swafford's *Johannes Brahms: A Biography* (1997) offers an excellent contextual overview of his life (though the psychological profile relies far too heavily on the now-discredited myth of Brahms the brothel pianist). In *Johannes Brahms: Life and Letters* (1997), Styra Avins lets the composer speak for himself through much of the surviving material, and offers a wealth of useful background information as well. Both books provided the quotations from Brahms' letters cited earlier, and both are well worth investigating. For your convenience, I list them once again in the bibliography.

On the purely musical side, however, options for the lay reader are far more limited. *Brahms: The Four Symphonies* (1996) by Walter Frisch contains some terrific information on the German symphony in the nineteenth century and on the contemporary reception of the individual works, but his analysis is highly technical and aimed primarily at scholars and performers well-versed in the arcane field of harmonic analysis. This of course is perfectly fine as far as it goes, but it's an approach that has always struck me as paying excessive attention to the details and intricacies of what we might call the music's plumbing and wiring. It tends to overstress the schematic design as seen on paper, rather than its realization in performance as living sound.

This is not to suggest that Frisch is in any way wrong in his approach. Harmony in Brahms is a richly fascinating topic, even if it remains one necessarily aimed more at an academic audience. His music responds particularly well to Frisch's method because the symphonies are chock full of musical devices that are analyzable and explicable in technical terms. Brahms himself was a musical scholar of profound learning, particularly on the subject of Renaissance and Baroque choral music, a great deal of which he performed during his periodic stints as a conductor. Yet another aspect of his engagement with history is that he witnessed, and participated in, the growth of musicology as an academic discipline, and counted among his friends most of the finest German musical scholars of the latter part of the nineteenth century.

Nevertheless, harmonic analysis is the least necessary and useful approach for most listeners because harmony and tonality (or "key") are basically self-explanatory as "what you feel as the music plays." They are the equivalent of color in painting, and you don't have to define "green," even assuming you could, in order to understand and enjoy an artist's use of it. In other words, harmony supports and conveys the music's expressive message, and you can describe that message perfectly accurately without having to get into either the details of what the harmony is doing, or the extent to which the composer's handling of it is intentional and systematic rather than instinctive or fortuitous.

For this reason, I think there's room for a popular, relatively jargon-free book on the symphonies that nevertheless seeks to explain them in musical terms. This does not mean asserting that everything you will hear is equally wonderful. The great English music scholar Donald Francis Tovey once famously remarked that the principal job of the writer of program notes is that of "counsel for the defense," stressing the importance of skating over imperfections in order to justify the time and effort the listener will spend listening to a long and complex work. The situation with Brahms, however, is somewhat different. We tend to take him for granted, and no one seriously challenges his greatness. Today, audiences are often too passively accepting, whether from cultural intimidation or simply in surrender to the music's surface prettiness.

I would like to take a different approach, and ask you to listen more closely. After all, Brahms doesn't need me (or anyone else) to defend him at this point in time; what he needs is listeners willing to engage the music actively and critically. If this means pointing out that Brahms' music does not have to be seen as uniformly successful in every aspect in order to merit the distinction of "greatness," or that you do not have to like all of it equally well (though of course you can if you so choose), then so be it. We should not let either Brahms avowed perfectionism or his subsequently being enshrined in the pantheon as one of the "Three Bs" (along with Bach and Beethoven) serve as an excuse for not considering his very real strengths and weaknesses. After all, it is the distinctive and *unequal* balance of elements that so often gives a work of art its special personality, and even accounts for much of its appeal.

Let's begin with this very basic fact: All symphonies are, first and foremost, compositions for the orchestra, and so our approach is going to focus on what the instruments do, based on the certain knowledge that you can learn just about all that you need to know from close listening to the music's melodic and timbral surface. In fact, this is exactly what Brahms expected, and it's primarily what his contemporaries, both amateurs and professionals, actually did. He held that nothing was more important than a good, strong melody effectively presented, and this principle underlies his love of everything from Strauss waltzes and gypsy bands to American ragtime and the vaudeville song "Tararaboomdeeay!"

One of the most pernicious myths in the classical music universe, evident to some extent even in Swafford's Brahms biography, is that contemporaneous audiences were supersophisticated in matters of musical form and syntax because, before the invention of radio broadcasting and sound recordings, most people either sang or played an instrument at home and thus had an innate understanding of the idioms and conventions of the period. Granted, there is no question that the ability to read and play music was necessarily more common back then than it is now, but it's a big stretch going from this factual observation to the assumption that nineteenth-century audiences had a greater understanding of the theoretical basis of musical composition in large forms.

On the contrary, the principal difference between audiences in Brahms' day and ours was not a function of musical education at all, at least not in the modern sense. If you read Brahms' letters, or leaf through critical writings in newspapers and published collections of essays, you will find virtually no discussion of the kinds of formal and technical matters that pepper even the most popular musical guides today. Almost no one mentions such specialized terms as "sonata form," "exposition," "recapitulation," and the like. They talk about beautiful, expressive melodies and affecting harmony, and they are often quite specific in noting if certain moments please more than others. But you will search in vain for any frequent or systematic theoretical discussion.

It is quite usual, for example, to see comments such as "the first theme is very beautiful, but the second is tiresome and really ought to be replaced with something more attractive." No one says "I understand the purpose of these ugly harmonies or that melodic digression and am happy to put up with them for the sake of the long-term architecture of the movement." Today's commentators start from the premise that in a musical masterpiece everything fulfills some purpose in the larger formal scheme, and they set out to prove it. Not surprisingly, most of the time they do just that, sometimes whether the music supports this thesis or not (happily Brahms' music almost invariably does).

Brahms' contemporaries couldn't have cared less about such matters, not just because his music had not yet entered the classical canon, but because they didn't see any need to "appreciate" or "understand" a new work in an especially effortful way. They merely took each piece as it came on the assumption that the composer always intended to please. Any less attractive parts, they felt, stemmed from the composer's failure at his primary job, and they had no compunction about saying so. It's no wonder that Brahms dreaded getting into musical discussions with just about everyone, his fans as much as his detractors. What drove him crazy was ignorance, and he didn't particularly care whether it arose from positive or negative feelings. To be ignorantly loved was, for him, just as irritating as being ignorantly despised.

For this reason, I would go so far as to suggest that serious music lovers today are just as well if not better equipped to enjoy Brahms as at any time in history—and today there are many more of them. At the very least they are much more prepared to consider a large work as a whole, listening intently and with respect, and this applies to contemporary music as much as it does the works of the acknowledged masters. Moreover, modern audiences are far more curious and willing to learn about how best to listen. They make greater demands of themselves and consequently have lower expectations of composers than at any time in the past. They understand and largely accept that their willingness to grant creators near total artistic freedom necessarily means developing a high threshold of tolerance, if not actual pain.

Nevertheless, nostalgia for the alleged loss of ancient musical utopias, defined as times when audiences craved modern novelties and understood them as part of a purportedly shared music language, infects many writers on musical subjects of all kinds, especially those who happen to be composers as well. It reflects their own need to feel relevant, their craving for acceptance, and it gives them an opportunity to vent their frustration at the museum mentality that favors the dead over the living in so much of today's musical culture. It ignores the vast amount of less formal or non-institutionalized musical activity going on today at every level: the countless amateur, professional, and semi-professional choirs, singers, bands, popular and classical music groups, not to mention the folk and ethnic ensembles that give our modern musical life such richness and texture.

I raise this issue here because one of the more harmful and common trends in the music appreciation business is the habit of trying to sell the product by insulting the intellectual and cultural preparedness of consumers. Sometimes this habit takes the form just discussed, of praising audiences of past eras. At other times, you may hear a lament about the lack of formal musical education in public schools. But as I have suggested earlier, there is no dearth of music in contemporary society; if anything there is too much. We are spoiled for choice, and what most classical music partisans are really complaining about is what they perceive as the lack of interest in the right *kind* of music. This problem assumes a particularly acute form in considering Brahms because he was both a very learned composer and a classicist, and for that reason his music has always excited the admiration of snobs.

Still, whatever Brahms' faults and personality quirks may have been, he was never a snob, either socially or musically. He learned music just as most people today still do: from individual instruction (in this case from his piano teachers), from private study, and ultimately from practical experience. In short, he was one of us. Many writers, comparing to our disadvantage the listening habits of audiences in earlier times, are far too ready to discount the real-life musical experience of the vast majority of people today—people who still acquire their knowledge exactly as Brahms did. The truth is that the classical music academic-industrial complex has always been deeply conflicted over its simultaneous craving for popularity and relevance, and a desperate, even disdainful insistence on preserving a monopoly on cultural superiority and privilege.

Obviously, this is not Brahms' fault. The bottom line is that there is absolutely nothing about his music that requires anything more from its audience than a willingness to listen and the time to invest in doing so. Quality in Brahms is synonymous with intelligibility. The greatest composers don't cultivate a belief in "hidden depths" that reveal themselves only to a select few, but ensure that their musical treasures lie on the surface, waiting to be noticed. Brahms would have considered this fact a simple question of competence, the logical outcome of his determination to be both true to himself and considerate to his audience. In accepting the responsibility that history imposed on him he shouldered a heavy burden, but as you will see and hear in the following discussion, he did so unflinchingly, and without question triumphantly.

Chapter 2

The Road to the Symphonies:
Brahms versus the Orchestra

BRAHMS HAD AN UNCOMFORTABLE relationship
with the orchestra. This isn't necessarily a bad thing. Triumph
over technical hurdles and the tension that the struggle creates is often good for art, and this is audibly true of the four
symphonies. Still, there's no question that Brahms was not
as gifted an orchestral writer as were his colleagues Wagner,
Tchaikovsky, Dvorák, or Bruckner. He knew it, and it both-
ered him. Nevertheless, the results he obtained were entirely
personal and, more to the point, appropriate to his view of
what "symphony" meant to him. In other words, it's a mistake to suppose that because others used the orchestra more
brilliantly than Brahms, he didn't know what he was doing,
or that all of his symphonic music sounds the same. Indeed,
if you listen to the thirteen purely orchestral works you will
discover not just considerable differences between them, but
that the symphonies have a special sound all their own, one
that's worth spending a little time trying to describe.

At the heart of Brahms' relationship with the orchestra lies his comment, previously cited, that a piece of music must have "not a note too much or too little, not a bar you could improve upon." If we take this statement seriously, and ask how Brahms applied it in practical terms, it's fair to say that as an aesthetic proposition it makes life much easier for a composer writing for the small ensembles typical of chamber music. This is because in a setting for limited forces, often with one instrument to each part, every note really can matter, and each one is meant to be heard. The orchestra, on the other hand, makes a virtue of redundancy. With multiple instruments to a part (especially strings) it exists, at least to some extent, simply to make a colorful noise. Indeed, much orchestral music can be reduced and transcribed for, say, a piano or small chamber group, without losing a single important note.

However, not all orchestral music can be rearranged in this fashion. Indeed, the best orchestral composers build instrumental timbre and dynamics into the formal architecture of the music itself, making it impossible to realize fully in any other medium. One of the most famous stories in the world of classical music concerns Liszt's boast to Mendelssohn that he could reproduce practically any orchestral texture with perfect fidelity on the piano. Mendelssohn replied: "If you can play the opening of Mozart's G-minor Symphony [No.40], I'll believe you." Mozart's symphony starts with divided violas playing a rapid rhythmic pattern that cannot be rendered with anything like its original timbral quality on a keyboard instrument.

Two other composers who exploited this principle to a very high degree were Haydn and Mahler. Brahms did not. For him, musical discourse can and often does exist as a thing apart from the instruments he chooses to present it. His symphonies generally work extremely well in the piano versions that he himself carefully prepared, however beautiful his orchestration may be. Similarly, the marvelously scored Haydn Variations are available in an equally valid version for two pianos. So is the thrillingly dramatic Piano Quintet in F minor. The First Serenade began life as a chamber work and only gradually achieved its final form as a self-conscious exercise in orchestration, while the First Piano Concerto (Brahms' first orchestral work) only became a concerto at all after taking shape initially as a sonata for two pianos.

However, the fact that Brahms was most comfortable writing chamber music, particularly when it included his own instrument, the piano, does not necessarily mean that his chamber works are more successful than his symphonies and concertos. The desire to make every note count also has risks of its own. It may, for example, encourage the composer to overwrite, to make his textures too busy just because the medium seems to encourage it. This is precisely what happens in the outer movements of Brahms' string quartets, and it explains why they tend to be respected more than they are loved (as well as why he only permitted three to be published out of the dozens that he claimed he actually wrote). His two string sextets, lovely works that even today aren't as well-known as they ought to be, are also sometimes accused of excessively heavy textures.

More to the point, Brahms was fully aware of the pitfalls and risks that his seriousness of approach and personal inclinations entailed, both in chamber and orchestral music. So although he wasn't the kind of composer to whom ideas came ready-made in their final, orchestral guise, he quickly found ways to force himself to think in orchestral terms. Consider, for example, the First Symphony's introduction. This hugely impressive exordium for full orchestra with pounding timpani simply doesn't translate well into any other medium, not even the piano. Brahms added it as an afterthought, a couple of decades after he began work on the first movement, and shortly before he permitted the symphony to see the light of day for the first time. It announces the arrival of "Brahms the symphonist" in an unmistakably orchestral way.

At the same time, we can't help but note that the most purely "orchestral" as well as picturesque ideas in the symphony (including the famous alphorn theme in the finale) occur in the introductions to the outer movements. In other words, once the dynamic process of development gets going, orchestral color becomes a secondary consideration. We can observe a similar phenomenon at work in the coda to the finale of the Third Symphony, some of the most ethereal and touching music he ever wrote, and purely orchestral to its core—but it happens after the principal body of the movement has run its course. Still, it's very important to keep in mind that "secondary consideration" does not mean "no consideration."

I also need to stress in this connection that this habit, using timbre and the special sound of the orchestra as a means of characterizing introductions or codas, really is a genuine point of style, part and parcel of Brahms' determination to ensure that every moment is "full of music," but only to the extent that is absolutely necessary and justifiable according to his own way of thinking. Introductions tend to be anticipatory, specifically of the remainder of the movement. Codas offer the chance to look back, whether calmly, joyously, sadly, or even tragically, on the terrain just traveled. In both cases, this means focusing attention on the vehicle that makes the musical journey possible, and in a symphony that vehicle is the orchestra itself. Furthermore, musical composition is not a zero-sum game in which the exploitation of one characteristic necessarily excludes another.

These observations say something significant about the kind of ensemble writing that Brahms finds appropriate to his symphonies as distinct from all of his other orchestral works. Although the basic Brahms orchestra isn't large by late Romantic standards (woodwinds in pairs, four horns, two trumpets, three trombones with bass reinforcement from tuba or contrabassoon, timpani, and strings), the sound he makes in the symphonies often comes across as surprisingly thick and rich. This stems principally from three further, complementary habits: an emphasis on middle and low instrumental registers; the clear predominance of the string section; and with only a few exceptions, a tendency to blend timbres and have whole sections play together, rather than write lengthy individual solos.

Brahms has the most problems with his orchestration when writing loud "tuttis," or sections when everyone plays together. The habits mentioned earlier create real problems of balance, while his restricted use of the brass risks making his climaxes sound inhibited, a problem that can be exacerbated by overly cautious interpreters treating his sometimes fussy score markings too literally. The human ear has an infallible ability to assess the dynamic potential of any instrument as a function of its basic timbre, and note a composer's failure to exploit it fully. It's probably fair to say that many of Brahms' most thrilling big moments occur when he is deliberately limiting his resources but at the same time using these resources to the maximum. The opening movements of the First and Fourth Symphonies, which omit trombones but still achieve a remarkably powerful sound, offer excellent examples.

In order to make these points even clearer, in the following pages you will find two charts, the first showing the scoring of all four Brahms symphonies movement by movement, and the second, for purposes of comparison, listing the scoring of the nine symphonies of his friend and colleague (and the only symphonic composer that he sometimes deemed his equal), Antonin Dvořák.

First, consider chart 1 of the Brahms symphonies. As you can see, one way that Brahms achieves contrast between movements is to score each of them slightly differently. Often, this means reducing the number of instruments in the lighter-textured inner movements, while reserving the largest forces for the first movements and finales. One fact that will become very clear on listening to the actual music is that whatever forces Brahms works with within a movement, he will use them frequently throughout. There are no "special effects" in his symphonic music, if by this we mean unusual timbres that make a single, surprising appearance for a bar or two and then disappear. Thus, although he only uses the triangle and piccolo in the third movement of the Fourth Symphony, he gives both of them very extensive parts. In short, everyone participates fully in the musical discourse, but not everyone necessarily plays in every movement.

Symphony:	No. 1				No. 2				No. 3				No. 4			
Movement:	1	2	3	4	1	2	3	4	1	2	3	4	1	2	3	4
piccolo															1	
2 flutes	X	X	X	X	X	X	X	X	X	X	X	X	X	X	1	X
2 oboes	X	X	X	X	X	X	X	X	X	X	X	X	X	X	X	X
2 clarinets	X	X	X	X	X	X	X	X	X	X	X	X	X	X	X	X
2 bassoons	X	X	X	X	X	X	X	X	X	X	X	X	X	X	X	X
contrabassoon	X	X		X					X			X			X	X
4 horns	X	2	X	X	X	2	3	X	X	2	2	X	X	X	X	X
2 trumpets	X	X	X	X	X	X			X	X			X	X	X	X	X
3 trombones				X	X	X		X	X	X		X				X
tuba					X	X		X								
timpani	X	X		X	X	X		X	X			X	X	X	X	X
triangle															X	
strings	X	X	X	X	X	X	X	X	X	X	X	X	X	X	X	X

Chart 1 Brahms Symphonies: Scoring by Movement

Second, note that all of the symphonies use either a tuba or contrabassoon, both "low" instruments, that contributes to a stronger, heavier bass line. In this respect Brahms shows a marked difference from Dvorák, who, as you can see in chart 2, uses piccolos frequently, as well as English horn, triangle, and even the harp. Furthermore, while Dvorák does write for the tuba, he never employs a contrabassoon. You might well ask how much any of these seemingly small details really matter, but you would be amazed at how telling these differences really can be, not just in and of themselves, but as indicators of other habits—such as Dvorák's

No.	Flute + Piccolo	Oboe + Eng. Horn	Clarinet + Bass Clar.	Bassoons	Horns	Trumpets	Trombones + Tuba	Perc.	Misc.
1	2+1	2+1	2	2	4	2	3		
2	2+1	2	2	2	4	2	3		
3	2+1	2+1	2	2	4	2	3+1	triangle	harp
4	2+2	2	2	2	4	2	3	triangle, bass drum, cymbals	harp
5	2	2	2+1	2	4	2	3	triangle	
6	2+1	2	2	2	4	2	3+1		
7	2+1	2	2	2	4	2	3		
8	2+1	2+1	2	2	4	2	3+1		
9	2+1	2+1	2	2	4	2	3+1	triangle, cymbals	

Chart 2   Dvořák Symphonies: Scoring (all works with strings + timpani)

much higher writing for violins and trumpets, or his love of the flute, all of which brighten his textures ever further.

Additionally, unlike Brahms, Dvořák frequently injects special tone colors into his music for brief periods. For example, the English horn in the Eighth Symphony only plays for a couple of bars in the first movement, but those are a solo version of the main theme, and they are placed so as to direct the listener's attention to that instrument's particularly evocative sound. The same observation holds true of the bass clarinet, which has a brief solo (again the main theme) only in the Fifth Symphony's finale. Indeed, as a general rule, what we tend to acknowledge as great (meaning highly colorful) orchestration rests to an extraordinary degree on the way composers handle their woodwind sections. This is because of all the members of the orchestra, the woodwinds have the most individual timbres, and can be used both alone and in any combination to create an almost limitless palette of tone color.

In practical terms, what really matters then is not so much how often or how many instruments are used, but how often instruments other than the strings get to play the tunes. The example of Dvořák's Fifth Symphony, composed in 1875, just one year before Brahms completed and premiered his First Symphony, is particularly instructive in this regard. The Dvořák opens with a fanfare for two clarinets, which is then repeated even more brightly by the flutes (with a little clarinet support). A quick, rhythmic crescendo then leads to the movement's principal theme, played by first violins doubled by trumpets and horns, over a leaping accompaniment in the trombones. The strings don't lead, and certainly don't dominate the texture, being limited to linking passages and rhythmic figures until they come into their own on the arrival of the graceful second theme.

All of this is very different from what you will hear in Brahms. In three of the symphonies, the first movement's main theme invariably goes to the violins. The odd man out is the Second Symphony, where the principal ideas appear in dialog between strings, horns, and woodwinds. Brahms almost never gives an important tune to the trumpets, and with very few exceptions uses his brass choir mainly as harmonic support. Furthermore, in all of the symphonies there are only four really noteworthy extended solos: for violin in the slow movement of the First Symphony, for horn in that same work's finale, another horn solo in the third movement of the Third Symphony, and the flute solo in the finale of the Fourth.

None of these passages have captured the popular imagination as have, say, the melody for horn in the slow movement of Tchaikovsky's Fifth Symphony, or the celebrated

English horn-led Largo of Dvořák's "New World" Symphony. There are, of course, countless lovely passages in the Brahms symphonies for wind instruments alone and in combination, particularly in his inner movements, and even a couple of dazzling brass licks (the closing bars of the Second Symphony), but ultimately almost all of the thematic heavy lifting, at least initially, goes to the violins and cellos. Again, these are not hard and fast rules, but tendencies and characteristics that snap into sharper focus in comparative listening between Brahms and other composers. It does not mean that Brahms' orchestration invariably sounds monochrome; but it does suggest that there is a clear instrumental hierarchy, with strings at the top level.

Perhaps the best way of understanding these points is to draw an analogy with painting, and particularly with Picasso and his so-called blue period. There's no question that his later, cubist works are sometimes more colorful in absolute terms, but that doesn't make them better, and many people prefer the "blue period" for its subject matter (often artists and acrobats) and more naturalistic handling of form. Nor does the overall emphasis on a single dominating color produce artistic tedium. Just the opposite: the result looks fascinating and new. In other words, on the assumption that the work is richly diverse in content, a restricted color palette can be a source of strength if it focuses the attention on other, equally important elements of the composition. So it is with Brahms.

That this kind of writing is specific to the symphonies can be demonstrated by glancing briefly at Brahms' other orchestral works. The First Serenade opens with a lively tune for solo horn, repeated and extended by clarinet and oboe.

The Second Serenade omits violins entirely, and uses a piccolo in its finale. Both works were composed with an ear toward exploiting woodwind sonority, and both are large works (six and five movements, respectively). But because of their emphasis on tone-color and comparatively relaxed demeanor, Brahms would not call them symphonies—despite their being richer in content and more tightly argued than many contemporaneous works by others that were so designated.

Similarly, Brahms was far more indulgent of orchestral solo possibilities in his concertos. The slow movement of the Second Piano Concerto features a prominent and very attractive cello solo, while the opening of the Violin Concerto's central Adagio, led off by a gorgeous oboe solo, is one of the orchestral woodwind section's great tests of artistry and musicianship, and one of the most noteworthy examples of such scoring since Mozart. The concerto format, which already features a principal solo instrument, naturally encourages contrast and dialog with the orchestra, both as a whole and with its individual members, and so Brahms obliges us accordingly. Finally, the Haydn Variations also displays an unusually wide range of coloristic variety because the sectional form benefits from the composer's characterizing each individual variation in contrast to all of the others.

These examples make it very clear that in crafting his symphonies Brahms was aiming for a different kind of sound—one certainly not lacking in vivid colors, but still somewhat distinct from what he found appropriate to music in other forms, and one particularly well-suited to the music's expressive message. Indeed, given the virtually limitless range of timbres available to the orchestral composer, the word that

most accurately sums up Brahms' technique in his symphonies is not so much "restrained," but rather "precise." There
are also some other reasons for the prominence that Brahms
gives to his string section, but instead of spending more time
discussing issues up front that will make far more sense in
the context of the actual music, let's consider this and any
remaining similar points in light of each symphony's individual personality.

Chapter 3

Symphony No. 1 in C Minor, Op. 68 (1876)

IN ORDER TO get the most out of your listening experience of Brahms' First Symphony, it's necessary to discuss one of the most intimidating aspects of classical music: form, and specifically "sonata form." This is arguably the most important invention in the history of Western instrumental music. You may recognize the term as it is most often used—to describe a piece of chamber music such as a piano *sonata*, violin *sonata*, Baroque trio *sonata*, and so forth. You may also have heard its textbook formal definition as a method of organizing a single movement into three or four main sections:

1. an "exposition" that presents two main subjects in their respective keys,

---

A bit of housekeeping: Each of the following chapters on the symphonies will first examine aspects of Brahms' style that are particularly applicable to the work at hand, and then describe the music in detail. If you're not interested in the introductory material, feel free to jump straight to the discussion of the individual movements.

2. a "development" that moves frequently through many keys ("modulates") as it works with this preexisting material,
3. a "recapitulation" that restates all of the music of the exposition in the initial or principal key,
4. and an optional wrap-up, or "coda," that provides a satisfying conclusion.

This generic description does not explain what sonata form is as much as it offers a description of its end results in certain instances. The reality is far simpler, infinitely more interesting, as well as more varied than the basic terminology suggests. As perfected by Joseph Haydn in the latter half of the eighteenth century, the best definition of sonata form is "dramatic motion through time." In other words, every piece in sonata form tells a story of feelings and emotions articulated as a chain of musical events, in which themes and motives act as the story's characters. Ultimately, Haydn expanded this notion to take in not just individual movements but entire works, meaning that it's really more accurate to think of sonata (which simply means "to sound") as a style or process rather than a specific form.

If we accept the notion of "sonata style" rather than "form," it is easy to understand that as the language of music changed between Haydn's day and Brahms's, a period of almost exactly a century, so the detailed treatment of form changed, even while maintaining the basic concept of "dramatic motion through time." You see, the beauty of the sonata style is its adaptability. Its ultimate shape and structure depends on the musical content that the composer creates in each individual work. Therefore it is incorrect to assert, as sometimes happens, that Brahms' use of sonata forms recalls that of the past classical masters because he was self-consciously imitating them. If there are parallels, they exist because the solutions to similar problems often produce similar results, and Brahms was one of the very few composers of his day who even recognized what the problems were, never mind how to solve them successfully.

The biggest issue a composer faces in creating a large, multi-movement work such as a symphony is how to convey the necessary feeling of onward motion, of starting in a specific place, departing from it and visiting other places in which "stuff happens," and then finally returning home (or somewhere equally satisfying), all in an emotionally gripping way. After all, if the job of a symphony merely was to present a sequence of expressively affecting tunes, it would all be over in a few short minutes, just like a song or other brief, lyrical piece. So to justify the length, variety, and complexity of a typical symphonic movement something has to happen to its themes (or "subjects" as they are more properly called).

Moreover, these happenings have to matter to us as listeners. They must be expressive, and we must be able to recognize and perceive each stage of the journey, no matter how surprising or unexpected it may be, as part of a larger, internally consistent, and logical scheme. You might well ask at this point why a composer can't just write music according to different formal principles entirely and forget about the sonata style? The answer is that doing so is practically impossible if the main goal remains achieving the richness and depth of expression that "dramatic motion through time" conveys.

Consider this analogy: If you want to travel from New York to California you can either walk or fly (or drive, or take a train). But if you want to do it in five hours while watching a movie or reading a book, then you have no choice but to fly. And so most people do just that, for reasons of efficiency, comfort, and convenience. Form in music really isn't that much different, in that one of its critical components is *time*. If you want to cram the widest possible range of emotional expression into a given time span, the sonata method simply works best. History has shown that it really does provide the foundation for most successful music in large forms, even in works that claim to follow a program—that is, some sort of external plotline derived from literature or an extra-musical idea.

A symphony then, by its very definition, is generally understood to mean "an orchestral work in the sonata style," and no composer who attempts one, even today, can avoid confronting the challenge of using sonata technique effectively. In Brahms' day this meant adopting either of two approaches, one easy, and the other far more difficult. The easy way is to treat sonata form as in the earlier textbook description, and simply fill up your three or four sections with attractive materials arranged according to the established rules (we don't need to go into those) governing the relationships between their respective keys or *tonalities*. Brahms' method, on the other hand, as well as that of certain other great symphonists of the Romantic period, including Tchaikovsky, Dvořák, Mahler, Sibelius, and Nielsen, is to let the material itself dictate its own formal shape, subject to the overall intent of creating "dramatic movement through time."

The difference between these two modes of operation might be likened to building a prefabricated house as compared to hiring a famous architect to produce a custom design.

Both can be perfectly livable, and of course much depends on the quality of the building materials. Just as there can be very expensive, attractive, and luxurious prefab houses, so too can there be wonderful symphonies whose ravishing melodies or brilliant orchestration conceal a somewhat stiff and unimaginative handling of form. This is what sometimes happens in the early symphonies of Tchaikovsky, Dvořák, and Bruckner, though at the end of the day it's the total package that counts most.

Brahms neatly avoided the problem of turning out immature work by withholding his First Symphony until he was sure he knew how to solve the motion problem to his complete satisfaction. There are no early Brahms symphonies, in fact no orchestral pieces at all in which potential formal problems have not largely been solved. This was one of Brahms' great strengths. Of course, as Brahms himself admitted in the statement that I quoted in the introduction, perfection of form doesn't always result in a beautiful work of art; that requires first-rate thematic material as well as the knowledge of how best to use it. So how did Brahms do it? And why was it such a thorny issue for a German composer in the Romantic period? These are precisely the questions that Brahms confronts in his First Symphony.

This work is a veritable manifesto on the art and science of creating "dramatic motion through time" in Romantic music. If we take a moment to understand some of the differences between this period and the preceding Classical period (roughly 1760–1830) it will be clear why this posed a particularly daunting challenge. Consider two elements: melody and harmony (or tonality). Classical composers, such as Haydn, Mozart, and Beethoven, followed what might best be called a "brick and mortar" approach to creating themes in their large works. Tunes tend to be short and catchy, and comprised of short rhythmic motives that can be detached and used to build new ideas clearly related to the original one. These are musical "bricks." Perhaps the most famous example in all of music is the opening theme of Beethoven's Fifth Symphony.

In addition, many very great movements, for example, much of the first movement and finale of Mozart's "Jupiter Symphony," use thematic material that is expressively neutral and not very distinctive—the "common coin" of the classical style. What makes the piece powerfully individual is the way the composer treats his material. The true possibilities of the themes only reveal themselves over the course of their development. I'm sure you can see very clearly how either strategy, alone or in combination, serves the cause of "dramatic motion through time" very well, because it throws the emphasis less on the individual character of the themes, however pronounced this may be, than on their potential to grow and evolve. Keeping some expressive potential in reserve for future development is one of the great secrets of Classical compositional technique.

In the Romantic period all of this changed, because the nature of Romantic melody was quite different. Tunes became longer, more obviously lyrical and song-like, and more self-evidently expressive on their face. Why this happened is a long and complex story, but it has a lot to do with the rise of domestic music-making in middle-class homes, a shift away from the swift, witty vocal style of comic opera in favor of heavy duty tragedy and melodrama, the compositional emphasis on art-songs and short "character" pieces,

the influence of ethnic nationalism, and the belief that composers needed to personalize their music so as to make their
own melodic style instantly identifiable. Brahms was himself
very much a composer in this new tradition. His most numerous works are songs—more than two hundred of them—and
as you will see his symphonies contain plenty of melodies of
notably songful quality.

The problem with writing long, beautiful melodies in the
sonata style is not so much that they can't be developed, but
that doing so risks making the music less expressive, not
more. As listeners, we naturally want to enjoy the Big Tune
in all of its pristine glory, and we rebel at hearing it taken
apart and "developed." Furthermore, highly lyrical music
often resists being played in fast tempos. It's very common
in both Classical and Romantic music to have a quick, energetic first subject in a sonata-form movement, and a more
relaxed, songful second subject (again, consider Beethoven's
Fifth). The need to slow down, or to give the impression of
slowing down, provides a welcome point of contrast when, as
in the Beethoven, the lyrical bits are relatively brief. But the
longer they become, the more they tend to sap the music's
forward momentum, breaking it up into a series of unrelated
episodes.

This is not a theoretical problem. If you want to hear a
particularly acute instance of a composer struggling with this
issue, consider the first movement of Rachmaninov's First
Symphony. It begins very impressively, with an energetic
first theme that soon peters out and comes to a complete
halt. The second subject is a very pretty, plaintive melody
in a totally different tempo that goes on for too long, and it
comes as a positive relief when the development opens with

a crash. Don't get me wrong: I love this piece, and in my opinion the music ultimately overcomes its somewhat dysfunctional form—but it's certainly touch-and-go for a while there, and the patient very nearly dies. In his much more famous Second Symphony, Rachmaninov figured out how to sustain momentum through his very long, lyrical second subject without compromising its melodic distinctiveness.

The second major problem confronting the Romantic composer in creating "dramatic motion through time" concerns the related subjects of harmony and tonality. These are, respectively, the short- and long-term manifestations of the same basic phenomenon, one which is very hard to describe verbally because it is an innately musical quality. Although an extensive technical vocabulary exists allied to the academic discipline of harmonic analysis, this is virtually useless in explaining how and why harmonic or tonal effects have an expressive impact on listeners as a function of long-term structure. We can explain *what* the composer does, but we cannot quantify precisely why it works so well or assess its comparative significance apart from other important musical elements.

However, it's very easy to describe (and hear) the basic differences between the Classical and Romantic periods in their handling of harmony and tonality as they relate to the sonata style, and to do so without recourse to complex technical terms. The very concept of telling a story through music without words presupposes three things: a beginning, a middle, and an end that are identifiable as such. One of the more remarkable things about a movement in sonata form is that you always know where you are in it; you actually can feel the music moving away from its starting point, perceive it traveling through different episodes, anticipate its return home, and look ahead to its final destination. The musical quality that permits this to happen is "tonality," or "key," and in particular the number of keys the themes visit, how long they spend in each one, and their relationship both to the main (or "tonic") key, and to each other.

Harmony, which is produced by combinations of notes played either simultaneously or over the course of a melody, in turn defines the key. In music of the Classical period, where the composer wishes to maximize this feeling of "dramatic motion through time," tonality is very strictly regulated. Themes must be chosen for their usefulness in revealing the keys that they initially inhabit. This is precisely why so many of them are based on simple chords and basic harmonies (again, Mozart's "Jupiter" Symphony offers a prime example). It is the audible contrast between keys, combined with a highly goal-directed method of "modulating," or moving between them, that gives Classical period music its unique energy and propulsion.

Accordingly, musical materials in the Classical period version of sonata style fall naturally into two broad categories: themes and motives that define specific keys (i.e., the "bricks" mentioned previously), and the often highly charged *motion music* that effects a transition between them (the "mortar"). However, by the Romantic period many of these distinctions had been abandoned. Composers, including Brahms, often preferred full-fledged "transition themes." You'll hear a particularly splendid one in the first movement of the Fourth Symphony. These may be quite beautiful and full of individual character. However, while some may increase the sensation of movement and energy while modulating between keys in vintage Classical style, just as often the music relaxes or seems to digress along the way to its next destination (as in the First and Third Symphonies).

This problem is compounded in the Romantic period by the music's higher level of dissonance and the frequent use of "chromaticism," or notes foreign to the basic scales that define the main tonality of a particular passage. For if harmony is the essential ingredient used to define a key, it can also be used just as easily to obscure or undermine one. The most famous essay in this subversive treatment of harmony is Wagner's opera *Tristan and Isolde* (1859), where chromaticism provides the perfect illustration of the title characters' intense (unto death), unfulfilled longing. Used strategically in Classical period works of Haydn, Mozart, and Beethoven, dissonance and chromaticism[1] create tension, further fueling the music's drive toward its ultimate harmonic resolution and providing the spice that prevents the larger tonal framework from turning dull.

However, the Romantic period's more pervasive use of dissonance and chromaticism, especially the latter, can either turn a piece of music into something almost unbearably expressive, or produce a quagmire of formless mush. Indeed, chromaticism at its most extreme is virtually synonymous

---

1. These two terms aren't quite identical. "Dissonance" is a technical term that refers to the use of notes outside of "consonant" chords and intervals that provide a stable, harmonious blending of tones. It's quite possible to be dissonant but not chromatic by sticking to the notes of the scale that define a particular key. For example, if you play all seven notes of a scale at the same time, you'll generate a whopping level of dissonance, but it will contain no chromatic tones at all. Similarly, you can create chromatic music that does not strike the ear as particularly dissonant (think of "cool" jazz), particularly today when we are quite used to such sounds.

with twentieth-century atonality. Most people hate atonality, not just because it often sounds ugly and inexpressive of anything other than pain, but because the lack of tonal contrast makes it very difficult to perceive musical structure. This in turn means that you never know where you are in the piece, why it's making the noises that you are hearing, and most importantly, how long it's going to last. Heightened expressivity has its price, though in the hands of a genius most would agree that the price is well worth paying.

For a good Romantic composer, taking advantage of the most recent compositional advances in harmonic practice was simply part of what it meant to be modern, and while much (too much!) is made of Brahms' regard for historical precedent and reverence for his precursors, when it comes to his handling of harmony and tonality he was one of the most advanced, if subtle, musicians of the period. This, then, was his mission: Write a symphony using the full resources of Romantic melody and harmony, in keeping with the Classical ideal of realizing to the highest degree the music's expressive potential as "dramatic motion through time."

Biographers like to define Brahms' own personal insecurity in historical terms, but I have gone into these points in such detail in the hope that you will also see the very serious musical challenge that he, and every other Romantic symphonist, truly faced. In a very real sense, the language of Romantic music worked against some basic elements of the sonata style as it was practiced in the Classical period. Successful realization of the symphonic concept required not adherence to tried and true formulas, but rethinking the problem from the ground up, and adapting the sonata style to the new material that it was asked to assimilate.

Complicating this task even further was the fact that a great many composers, critics, and academics pedantically insisted on adherence to a series of alleged Classical "rules" of form. For them, the sonata style was not a process, but an unchanging musical structure consisting of distinct components—that prefab house I just mentioned. Although they claimed to be supported in their view by historical precedent, what really motivated their thinking was the need to find a foolproof vehicle to contain and focus the new, highly expressive, but comparatively directionless Romantic melody, harmony, and tonality. Still, the fact remains that the Classical masters did not follow establish patterns; they created new ones, and so did Brahms.

If this discussion is correct, then, in asserting that the form of a movement in Brahms arises naturally from its melodic content, it pays to consider his themes, and how he handles them, very closely. Those in the first movement of the First Symphony belong among the most chromatic, un-lyrical, purposefully ugly, but also emotionally intense that he ever wrote. Even today they tend to sound "modern" in a partly negative sense. Expressively speaking this is a turbulent, angry piece, a fact that led to the First Symphony's being met with a certain amount of popular disapproval among contemporary audiences. The high level of dissonance and harmonic instability inherent in the material itself means that achieving a Classical sort of goal-directed, forwardly propulsive musical argument will be particularly difficult.

In this sense, Brahms is already stacking the deck against himself, although the motion problem is mitigated somewhat by the fact that agitated, rhythmically angular music works well at a quick basic tempo. A lesser composer might contrast an angry, truculent first subject with a mellow and relaxing second theme, providing a welcome contrast in tone and offering a point of harmonic repose, even if this tends to kill the music's forward momentum. This is not Brahms' solution here, perhaps because he has not yet figured out how to incorporate large tracts of lyrical music into a symphonic sonata-allegro scheme, but more importantly because the emotional climate of his first movement doesn't require them. That will be a task accomplished in the Second Symphony.

Here on the other hand, the use of extreme material within the sonata style naturally gives rise to an extreme formal approach. Accordingly, this is Brahms' only symphonic first movement in what has come to be called "monothematic sonata form." There is no melodically independent second subject at all. Furthermore, every single idea in the exposition arises quite audibly from the themes and motives that you hear in the introduction. The result has an unprecedentedly powerful, obsessive, indeed relentless intensity of expression, qualities nowhere better illustrated than by the steadily pounding timpani strokes that underpin the symphony's opening measures.

As with so many aspects of sonata form, the monothematic variety was invented by Haydn, most famously in the first movement of a work that Brahms hugely admired: Symphony No. 88 in G major. As used by his illustrious predecessor, monothematicism means that the movement is "front loaded." The business of exposition, to the extent that this means "presentation of material," is compressed to allow the maximum amount of expressive development in a relatively brief span of time (Haydn was always an extremely concise composer). More importantly, the music begins evolving almost immediately, blurring the usual division of a typical sonata-form movement into separate exposition and development sections.

For Brahms, however, as for most Romantic composers, the issue is quite different. He's working on a much larger scale than Haydn. The first movement of the First Symphony is about double the length of a comparable eighteenth-century work, and it would be difficult to imagine music more immediately passionate than its introduction and first subject. So for Brahms, the challenge lies in *sustaining* the emotional intensity that he establishes at the outset, while finding sufficient internal contrast to produce the necessary variety of dramatic events. The use of monothematic sonata form helps Brahms to shape his exposition as a single unified span, and in so doing it also goes a long way in solving the long-term motion problem.

First Movement: Un poco sostenuto—Allegro
[A little sustained—Quick]
Scoring: pairs of flutes, oboes, clarinets, bassoons, and
trumpets, one contrabassoon, four horns, timpani, and
strings

Brahms' heading over his first movement introduction, "a little sustained," recalls the similar marking at the start of Beethoven's Seventh Symphony, and is just as ambiguous. It really isn't a tempo indication at all, but more one of general character, and this in turn suggests that this theoretically "slow introduction" shouldn't be played all that slowly. Accordingly, two different performance traditions arose: the huge, majestic, granitic approach, with the timpani pounding away like the crack of doom, and a more lithe, urgent, and propulsive view that anticipates more obviously the allegro to come. The former tradition is best exemplified by those "grand old men" of the German school, Otto Klemperer and Wilhelm Furtwängler. The latter style characterizes performances by Arturo Toscanini, Günter Wand, and the "historical performance" movement (best represented by Charles Mackerras).

However it's played, this introduction represents one of the most impressive opening gestures in all of symphonic music. Once you know the music well, you will also realize that it could only have been written after the completion of the rest of the symphony, for what Brahms has done is to take the music of his entire first movement exposition, which as previously mentioned he worked very hard to make continuously propulsive, and break it up into discreet chunks. What appears in the allegro as a continuous idea given to the violins at high volume here is presented in dialog, with constantly changing textures and dynamics. It's a sign of just how much music Brahms packs into a mere two-and-a-half–three minutes that the introduction sounds, if not necessarily longer, then somehow much bigger that its relatively brief duration might suggest.

The result not only has its own distinct form (ABAC), but it achieves the critical goal of letting you get a sense of the main ideas without upstaging their formal presentation when the allegro finally gets going. The initial "A" section features those famous pounding timpani, and a rising chromatic phrase in the violins clashing with a wailing, descending line in the winds. "B" is a quiet and mysterious dialog between woodwinds (with pizzicato accompaniment) and the full string section. A crescendo over throbbing timpani leads back to "A," only this time the kettledrums have a roll instead of individual notes, leading to a plaintive oboe solo that serves as a transition to the allegro. Cellos echo the oboe's melody, and the introduction comes to a full stop, pianissimo.

Donald Francis Tovey argued with good reason that the start of the Allegro, had it not been preceded by the introduction, would have constituted one of the most abrupt openings in all of symphonic music, and this fact alone goes a long way toward explaining why Brahms felt it necessary to alter his original concept. Pay particular attention to the rising three-note motive in the woodwinds immediately following the initial jolt. It's hugely important throughout the first movement and even beyond. The violins take over from the winds, and the music surges forward along the lines just described in considering the movement's form. Two additional motives contribute significantly to the "first subject": the leaping theme in the strings that together with the three-note woodwind motive constitute "A" from the introduction, and the orchestral answer with downward swoops from violins, which you may recognize as the introduction's woodwind/string "B" section.

Although discussions of form in the abstract may be confusing at first, it's important to keep in mind that the reason it exists is to organize the music in an expressively clear way. There are no "hidden depths" here—just the opposite. Accordingly, Brahms follows up his first subject with what's called in musical parlance a "counterstatement," which is just a technical way of saying "he repeats the tune all over again," usually with different scoring and contrasting dynamics. The most common form of counterstatement consists of a loud repetition for full orchestra of an initial quiet theme, as you can hear at the start of Beethoven's "Eroica" Symphony. Brahms goes the opposite route, that is, loud to soft, at least initially, and scores it for lower strings rising swiftly to a climax for the full ensemble.

Hearing the first subject once again not only helps you to get the tunes into your memory, it reveals the music as already starting the process of "development," as the repetition isn't quite literal, and the continuation must necessarily be different to effect a transition to the next section. As the music settles down to a state of uneasy calm, a brief pizzicato bridge passage introduces the second subject—a very clever rearrangement of all the motives presented thus far with very different scoring, dynamics, and harmony (a soothing major tonality predominates). The oboes, in particular, have a plaintive melody based on "B" of the introduction, here given to woodwinds so that the tone color jogs your memory. Oboe, clarinet, and horn then bring the music to a near standstill on alternating repetitions of the first few notes of the allegro's initial theme.

Suddenly the violins begin muttering a descending, three-note motive in a rapid crescendo that extends the figure to four notes in a manner that may recall the famous "fate" motto from Beethoven's Fifth. If you pay attention to the arc of the melody by focusing on the accented fourth, long note, you may catch that fact that what you are actually hearing is a stretched-out ("augmented") version of the three-note idea that opened both the introduction and the allegro proper. Brahms works this up into an excitingly jagged climax that bounces its way to a jerky, two-note dialog between strings and winds, leading either back to the beginning of the exposition or straight into the development (in performances without the repeat, this usually occurs somewhere around the six–six-and-a-half minute mark).

I have to confess that I'm of two minds regarding this particular optional repeat. It's not one of Brahms' better prepared moments, sounding somewhat arbitrary in performance, and the music is so thematically economical and highly developed already that little seems to be gained in going back to the start of the allegro once again. On the other hand, this same fact—that so much development has already gone on—can be used to argue in favor of clarifying the movement's form by taking the repeat and letting the listener know exactly where the development starts. It's very much a matter of personal choice, and thanks to recordings [particularly Jochum/EMI, Giulini/Los Angeles (DG), or Mackerras (Telarc)] you have the option of hearing the music either way and judging for yourself.

The development section begins fortissimo with the strings playing a richly harmonized version of the allegro's opening theme, quickly subsiding to pianissimo, where the same tune appears in a mysterious, augmented (longer-note) version on lower strings and bassoons underpinned by throbbing timpani strokes. This leads, almost exactly as at the end of the exposition, to the passage with the "Beethoven's Fifth" motive, and to perhaps the most wonderful moment in the entire movement. Brahms interrupts this stormy outbreak with a serene chorale for the strings cloaked in pure, unclouded major-key harmonies. The material is entirely new. Some commentators have attempted to trace it back to the exposition, but the entire point of the passage is that it should come as a complete surprise and stick out like a searchlight cutting through the evening darkness.

This passage triumphantly solves a genuine aesthetic problem: in a movement that has already developed its principal material so extensively, what more is there to do? How can Brahms create the necessary drama and tension if he's limited to recycling the same material over and over? Clearly a greater range of contrast is required, and so Brahms supplies it here. The chorale vies with the Beethoven motto for supremacy, but the presence of the latter both thematically and as a rhythmic accompaniment to the chorale foreshadows the ultimate outcome. Darkness prevails, and the music subsides into another mysterious episode featuring the Beethoven motto repeated over and over on timpani against the first few notes of the introduction on violins and woodwinds.

The remainder of the development section is essentially a huge gesture of preparation for the return of the first subject. It's based almost entirely on the symphony's opening (which equals the three-note motive that launched the allegro). Brahms builds this in a long, slow crescendo starting with lower strings and contrabassoon, over which the clarinets hint at the Beethoven motive. At the height of the crescendo, the full orchestra comes crashing in, trumpets and timpani hammering out the "fate" rhythm with fanatical persistence, and rising in chromatic waves aimed squarely at the distant shore of the home key of C minor. But Brahms has another surprise in store: the music seems to "overshoot" its target, pausing on a couple of loud chords to survey the horizon, before executing a stunning about-face to arrive with all the more impressive finality at the recapitulation.

Brahms' handling of this passage is one of those moments that really tests your feeling for tonal relationships. It's entirely possible that you won't hear what I have just described at first, or if you already know the symphony, perhaps you never thought to notice anything unusual going on. It really does depend on developing a sense of how the sonata style operates, and because it's a perceptual issue it can't really be taught or even fully described. It has to be felt. My own personal experience suggests that with time you will begin to notice these details if you don't already; the music essentially explains itself the more familiar it becomes, and that's one of the things that's so wonderful about the classics in general. Close acquaintance only makes them more interesting, never less.

The recapitulation is mostly regular, another result of there having been so much development going on from the start. The only major difference is that Brahms omits the first subject's counterstatement (we've heard that tune enough!), and instead goes straight to his second group, which appears complete, although with numerous refinements in orchestral detail. The stormy passage featuring the Beethoven motive now expands into a more climactic episode and so initiates the coda. This begins with the symphony's opening three-note motive played both right side up and upside down (inverted), like a series of exhausted sighs after a long and difficult struggle. The Beethoven motive on the timpani underpins the whole passage, until one last reference to the allegro's main theme steers the movement into port with a calm and hugely welcome wash of C major tonality.

The fact that I am able to describe several minutes of music, the recapitulation and coda, pretty completely in a single paragraph, tells us something very important about the sonata style as it applies to this movement. The purpose of the recapitulation and coda is to give you a feeling of "return," of "coming home." Brahms achieves this in two ways: literal repetition, which gives a feeling of familiarity, and stability of tonality, which leaves the music rooted in the same place whereas previously it gave evidence of wanting to go elsewhere. This latter quality concerns the second subject particularly, because this is the music that established the movement's subsidiary keys and thus represented the first step on the journey away from "home."

This is precisely why Brahms offers us the full second subject—that and the fact that the most recognizable elements of the first subject comprise the melodic substance of the coda. The soft major-key ending however, so perfectly appropriate emotionally, might also come as a surprise after so much storm and stress. After all, the first movement of Beethoven's Fifth, in so many ways Brahms' model here, maintains its stern concentration on the minor key right up to the last note. Indeed, Brahms' ending asks a question that some listeners may feel isn't entirely resolved by the end of the finale, and we'll address this issue in considering that movement. Still, it's hard not to hear this glowing final chord as Brahms' own audible sigh of relief that his First Symphony had surmounted its first major challenge.

Second Movement: Andante sostenuto [Sustained
moderate (walking) tempo]
Scoring: Same as first movement, but only 2 horns

The size of the first movement and finale in this symphony tend to relegate the inner movements to a supporting role, even more so than usual. Brahms never was one to write a big symphonic adagio (meaning a long movement in very slow tempo) such as Bruckner regularly produced, or the emotionally supercharged effusion of sweeping melody that Tchaikovsky favored. His slow movements tend to be inti-mate, often almost conversational in tone, and never unusu-ally large in scale. While never lacking emotional depth or melodic character, their moods tend to emphasize the gentle, elegiac, and (occasionally) mysterious, with sudden gusts of passion.

Formally this andante is quite simple: ABCA. Originally it was longer. There was another statement of the "A" sec-tion between "B" and "C," but Brahms cut this out prior to publication, enhancing the music's expressive urgency. Even a composer as hardworking and discriminating as Brahms often needs to hear a new work in actual performance to get a feel for its optimal form. In the days before record-ings it's difficult to underestimate just how important these all-too-infrequent opportunities must have been. Playing the piece through on the piano isn't quite the same thing, since successful (meaning, not boring) forms in orchestral music depend both on memory and the kind of timbral contrast that can only be achieved hearing them as scored.

The "A" section has been aptly described as a kind of "musical prose." There is no real tune or extended melody, but rather a series of phrases for the violins having the ebb and flow of clauses in a long sentence. The third of these makes open reference to the symphony's first bars—that three-note figure that also introduced the allegro. The effect of the whole lengthy idea is very charming and innocent, and perhaps even a touch shy. A bit over a minute into the move-ment, a solo oboe interjects the closest thing to a complete melody that we have heard so far, a tune that most listeners tend to remember when recalling the movement as a whole. This breaks off as the strings conclude the opening section and lead without pause into "B."

Because Brahms conflated his two middle episodes, there's a lot of variety in the next couple minutes of music. The section begins with a lovely melody for the first violins over a regular accompaniment in so-called dotted rhythm (dum, dadum, dadum, etc.). This rhythm also featured quite prominently in the first movement, and if you pick this up then all to the good—it may or may not be an intentional point of resemblance. As the volume increases along with the weight of scoring, the accompaniment becomes heavier, even menacing, and the pathos of the melody deepens similarly, veering in the direction of minor-key harmony. This in turn perfectly sets up section "C," which begins in the minor with another oboe solo over a different rhythmic figure in the strings. It arises so naturally from the previous section that you'd never know that they weren't originally joined together.

This oboe solo, followed by the clarinet, is less an independent melody than a sort of ornamental arabesque. It may be that Carl Nielsen had this passage in mind in writing the somewhat similar wind solos in the slow movement of his own Third Symphony a few decades later. The entrance of the clarinet seems to usher the music in a brighter harmonic direction, but the lower strings get a hold of the clarinet's arabesque and once again the mood darkens as the full string section weighs in with a brief but passionate outburst. On the other side of this climax, after some quiet, broken phrases tossed back and forth between the woodwinds and strings, listen very carefully for the pianissimo entrance of the timpani, which signals the return of "A."

In the first movement, you will recall, Brahms took some care to keep his recapitulation regular. This movement's greater formal simplicity imposes no such constraint, and he recomposes his "A" section quite extensively, greatly enriching the scoring, varying the phrases, and adding attractive ornamental touches (such as the pizzicato runs that introduce the third phrase recalling the symphony's opening). The oboe solo gets assigned to a solo violin in the most extended passage of its kind in any of the symphonies. This solo needs to be played with a certain unsentimental purity, and while I'm no fan of the current (and completely wrong) orthodoxy that holds that Romantic string music in the latter half of the nineteenth century should be played with very little vibrato, there's no question that restraint is called for here lest the passage turn saccharine.

The solo violin also features prominently in the coda, a delicious episode accompanied by "heartbeats" in the timpani and strings. Brahms offers a series of gentle recollections of previous ideas (especially the symphony's opening three-note motive), and a touch of the "A" section's accompaniment too. Take care to notice the presence of the timpani in the final measures. Brahms' handling of the kettledrums, as with his brass writing, is often fastidious to the point of excessive caution, but he really did understand just how lovely this very limited instrument could sound in a quiet context, and he takes full advantage of this special tone color in bringing the movement to a most poetic close, solo violin on high.

Third Movement: Un poco Allegretto e grazioso
[A little bit quick and graciously]
Scoring: full orchestra minus contrabassoon, trombones, and timpani

The literal English translation of this delightful movement's tempo designation would probably be closer to: "a little bit moderately quick and graciously," but I have simplified
it to eliminate the redundancy. Brahms was famous for coming up with extremely detailed tempo designations. Haydn
and Beethoven between them invented the movement type
knows as the scherzo ("joke"), a swift piece in triple time and
having an ABA form, often featuring lots of rhythmic sur-
prises. For his first three symphonies Brahms created a kind
of scherzo substitute, an intermezzo in moderate tempo for
reduced orchestra, often giving the woodwind section an
opportunity to shine.

This particular example is in duple meter (2/4) for the
simple reason that the preceding Andante was already in 3/4
time, while the first movement was in 6/8 (compound meter,
which for our purposes counts as triple in terms of rhythmic
suppleness and lightness). It has a special form: ABACA-
coda(C). You may see section "C" called a "Trio," which in
this context simply means "middle section." The term is very
old, and usually gets used in association with dances (minuets), marches, or scherzos. For example, the famous "gradua-
tion theme" from Elgar's *Pomp and Circumstance March No. 1*
is technically a trio, as is the equally well-known melody with
its brilliant piccolo descant from Sousa's *Stars and Stripes
Forever*.

Normally in Classical period symphonies the initial "A"
part of a scherzo has two sections, both repeated: aabb, as
does the trio. Brahms' "C" section does have one big repeat
as well as a change of key and time signature (to 6/8), and
for this reason it often earns the "trio" designation in discussion of the piece, even though the movement's actual form

is a bit more sophisticated than that of a traditional scherzo. However, it may just be easier to describe the movement as a "rondo," which also happens to correspond exactly to the ABACA shape. I'm going into the formal issues that this outwardly simple movement raises simply to show that even when he's writing on a small scale, and very *grazioso*, Brahms never for a minute sacrifices his fundamental structural originality.

This same observation applies to the clarinet's opening melody, whose second phrase is an inversion (upside-down copy) of its first. Few composers used supposedly learned devices with as much ease and expressivity as Brahms, and this particular example offers telling proof. Flutes join clarinets and bassoons in the melody's gently lilting second half, a sequence of descending scales in dotted rhythm. I should mention at this point that some commentators, including Walter Frisch, regard the principal idea's second-half scales as an independent theme in its own right, and subdivide the opening "A" section into a series of melodic pairs: ABA'B'CDC'D'A". I have to say that this strikes me as unnecessarily complicated and formulaic, as well as contrary to the unity of the opening tune as I hear it, but you may certainly disagree.

Brahms immediately offers a piano counterstatement of the opening melody on the violins, with the clarinet providing a bucolic counterpoint in triplets [often not brought out sufficiently in performance; Solti (Decca) and Jochum (EMI) are both excellent here]. The woodwind "answer" is scored almost identically as before, but now the strings take over and lead the harmony toward a more anxious minor key (but still, always, *grazioso*!), and the "B" section. Once again the clarinet leads, this time atop a palpitating string accompaniment, and once again the massed woodwinds respond with the tune's second half. A variant of "B" on solo oboe in dialog with the strings leads swiftly back to the opening melody, but it only gets as far as its first half before evaporating into the trio section ("C").

This is a melody that has a shape that Brahms is going to exploit very extensively in the Second Symphony—three motives or phrases arranged: aab. Little "a" consists of a three-note call on the woodwinds answered by three descending notes from the strings in the same rhythm. This is immediately repeated. Little "b" is a rollicking woodwind phrase that clearly spells out the section's 6/8 rhythm. The whole idea only take a few seconds to play. This gets tossed back and forth between various orchestral sections in a big crescendo that even has the trumpets getting a shot at "b"—another moment that needs to be brought out a bit more than some conductors will permit. With typically Brahmsian caution, the trumpets are only marked forte to the woodwinds' fortissimo, but the passage really benefits from being able to hear their brassy timbre. The crescendo gets repeated exactly, before strings and woodwinds make the transition back to "A."

As is so often the case with Brahms, the transition becomes a particularly wonderful moment. The clarinet begins its initial melody, but the flute supplies a new counterpoint in the form of "b." The violins then take over and extend the tune with a clear foreshadowing of the second half of the "Big Tune" to come in the finale. This is one of those points that you really only come to notice once you know the symphony, at which point it may well become an eagerly anticipated event. After the melody's second-half descending scales, all reharmonized to create a wonderfully nostalgic mood, a last reference to the trio section brings the movement to a punctual but serene close.

Finale: Adagio—Più Andante—Allegro non troppo,
ma con brio [Slow—more moderately—quick;
not too fast, but with verve]
Scoring: full orchestra, with trombones for the first time

Before considering the music of the finale in detail, it's necessary to examine it in light of one of the most interesting and frustrating questions, for composers at least, in the aesthetics of musical Romanticism. It's called "the finale problem," and it's defined as the difficulty in creating a convincing ending that makes a grand statement and resolves the symphony's preceding tensions without ever sounding boring, hollow, bombastic, tacky, or contrived. It's a particular issue in works that are "bottom heavy," having finales that constitute the weightiest (and often longest) movement in the whole symphony. Composers were well aware of this issue, and agonized over it. There were classical precedents: Mozart's "Jupiter" Symphony and Haydn's Symphony No. 98 offer two examples, but the real challenge was handed down by Beethoven in his Fifth and Ninth Symphonies.

In this Beethovenian form, the problem applied specifically to heroic works that begin in tragic, minor keys and conclude joyously in the major. Even Beethoven wasn't given a free ride by critics in Brahms' day. The finale of his Ninth Symphony remained controversial for its introduction of voices (an aesthetic "copout" insisted some critics, Brahms' best journalistic friend Eduard Hanslick among them), but that of the Fifth was in Brahms' time considered basically beyond reproach, and in any case he knew perfectly well the models to which his finale was going to be compared, rightly or wrongly. That is why, when someone pointed out the resemblance between this finale's Big Tune and Beethoven's "Ode to Joy," he supposedly snapped back, "Any fool can see that!"

The reason the classical composers didn't have to face a "finale problem" in the same way the Romantic composers did has to do with two issues: form, and scale. Classical works in sonata form are generally top heavy: the first movement is the largest, and the remaining ones tend to explore less rigorous forms, which means that they are also usually shorter. Beethoven's Fifth and Ninth Symphonies, though, are bottom heavy; their biggest movements are their finales. That of the Fifth Symphony is in full blown first movement sonata form, and it's attached to the scherzo—linked to it thematically and motivically—making for a truly huge structural complex. The Ninth Symphony concludes with a theme and variations, one that not only includes voices, but introduces them with a verbal explanation by Beethoven himself of exactly what it proposes to do: "*Oh friends, not these sounds, etc.*"

The job for the Romantic composer was made all the more difficult thanks to the era's love of melodramatic expression. In music, this means a penchant for minor keys and the expression of sad, pathetic, angry, or tragic emotion. Consider these statistics: Beethoven wrote two symphonies in minor keys (of nine), Mozart two (of more than sixty), and of Haydn's most famous batch, the twelve last "London" symphonies, only one adopts a minor key as "home" (No. 95), and it's one of the least popular. Brahms, on the other hand, planned two of his four symphonies around minor keys, Dvořák four (out of nine), Bruckner five (out of nine numbered works), and Tchaikovsky five (out of six). In the Russian composer's case, it is his single major key work (Symphony No. 3 "Polish") that is his least popular and successful.

These are remarkable figures, particularly when you consider that at all periods tragic endings for abstract instrumental pieces were virtually unheard of. There are only four late-Romantic symphonies of note that end in minor keys: Brahms' Fourth, Tchaikovsky's Sixth, Mahler's Sixth, and Sibelius' Fourth. Even Felix Draeseke's portentously titled "Symphonia tragica" (Symphony No. 3), a popular work in its day that Brahms knew and admired, ends in seraphic tranquility. So a work that deals with "big issues" needs an optimistic finale worthy of them, a tall order in any circumstances, and particularly in an era in which the Classical period's musical saving grace, namely, a sense of humor, was notably absent.

A love of melodrama, of dwelling on emotional gloom and angst, goes hand in hand with a taste for grandiosity. The nineteenth century was the great era of nation building, of industrialization, and of mass political movements. These trends naturally affected the arts. Even Brahms, the theoretical arch-classicist, was working on a very large scale by classical standards, and a sixteen minute (or so) finale like that of the First Symphony still stands out today as very ambitious. The Romantic period is full of long, lousy finales: rhythmically stiff, boring, monotonous exercises in the mechanics of form, emotionally empty and expressively unconvincing. This certainly is not one of them. Brahms always masters his forms, and his handing of it here is particularly well-knit and ingenious.

However, you might well be justified in feeling that Brahms doesn't quite address a specific, less generic expressive problem that he created for himself. Namely, the first movement ended in such a mood of "all passion spent," and the next two movements offered interludes of almost consistently idyllic character that in order to create a "tragedy to triumph" finale he needs to contradict the ending of the first movement and return to square one: the turbulent atmosphere with which the symphony began. This he does, risking the possibility of the listener saying "I thought we were over and done with that!" But in reality he has no choice, given the sequence of moods presented thus far. Every listener must determine individually the degree to which he succeeds. A lot depends on the conductor in pacing not just the finale, but the entire work.

The structure of Brahms' finale is sometimes described as "sonata form without development." Like most such descriptions, this can be misleading. What really happens is that a formal "development section" is absent from its usual place. Instead, it's moved to the transition between the first and second subjects, and is often then based entirely on the former. This was a favorite device of Mozart's, particularly in slow movements. One of the great twentieth-century symphonists, Czech composer Bohuslav Martinu also used it extensively (consider the first movement of his Symphony No. 4), perhaps following Brahms' example here.

Atop this larger formal structure, elements of the movement's lengthy introduction turn up with increasing frequency as the finale proceeds, transformed into new themes and also as originally heard. This process of integration, of bringing what was once tense and gloomy into the orbit of the happy and joyful, builds on the resolution achieved at the end of the first movement, only in a more dynamic and definitive way. Brahms further avoids that undesirable "Been there, heard that" feeling by adopting a couple of specific strategies, and in order to consider these we now turn to the music in detail.

The first thing you might notice about the finale is that it begins with a descending phrase for cellos, basses, and contrabassoon quite similar to the one that concluded the previous movement, only slower in tempo. This, plus the mysterious harmonies that follow, gives the music a feeling of being already in progress, a conversation picked up in mid-stream. Without formally linking the third movement to the fourth, as Beethoven does in his Fifth Symphony, Brahms thus achieves a similar continuity. Many live performances enhance this further by starting the finale after only a very short pause. This is less evident on recordings where the gap between movements is often determined in post-production editing. One version with a notably brief pause is Abbado's with the Berlin Philharmonic (DG). You might want to try experimenting at home to see how changing the length of this between-movement gap affects your perception of the finale's opening gesture.

Violins and woodwinds (flutes, oboes, bassoons) immediately follow the initial descent-plus-timpani-crescendo with a bit of melody that later turns out to be the first notes of the Big Tune, though the resemblance is much easier to see on paper than it is to hear. The orchestra dies down to a most unusual and creepy passage for pizzicato strings, *accelerando* (accelerating), in little two-note bits. You may have noticed that Brahms is very partial to pizzicato, especially in transitional material, and he's equally fond of tunes made out of two-note links of musical chain. We already heard one in the transition between first and second subjects in the first movement. Is this a distant recollection of that earlier event?

Brahms then repeats the whole opening sequence, but in a slightly compressed form to increase the urgency. This time, shuddering strings and a climbing motive in the woodwinds lead to a wonderfully windswept passage for sighing violins, rushing to a climax harmonically (but not melodically) based on the symphony's opening three-note motive as heard at the end of the first movement exposition. Notice how delicately Brahms alludes to music heard previously, avoiding literal repetition as if to say "We are not going back—but the memory, or nightmare, is still with us." Then, with a crash on the timpani, the clouds part and salvation beckons in the form of the alphorn theme that Brahms quoted in his famous letter to Clara Schumann.

Played by French horn followed by a solo flute marked, somewhat optimistically in my view, *forte sempre e passionato* [always loud and passionate], and accompanied by a shimmering halo of strings, Brahms establishes the two opposite expressive poles that the finale proper will proceed to bridge. As the alphorn theme subsides, the three trombones make their first entrance in the entire symphony playing a solemn chorale, as if from afar. This can be a very nerve-wracking entrance, evidenced by the famous blooper committed by the Philharmonia Orchestra's principal trombone in that ensemble's famous live Brahms cycle under Toscanini (Testament).

One more round of alphorn from the winds entering in over-lapping sequence, and the finale proper is finally ready to get underway.

Although the themes in this finale fall into the usual first and second subjects of a sonata form exposition, the way you really hear them is closer to a grand pageant or procession of individual ideas, again as in the finale of Beethoven's Fifth Symphony. So the easiest way to follow the course of the music is simply to list the tunes in order:

1. First Subject: The Big Tune, played first by all the upper strings with pizzicato accompaniment, then by the full woodwind section, with timpani added to the plucked strings. This tune may have been inspired by Beethoven, but it had a huge influence on the finales of later composers from the ridiculous (Hans Rott Symphony No. 1) to the sublime (Nielsen Symphony No. 3 "Sinfonia Espansiva"). Brahms immediately follows this twofold repetition with a forte variation for full orchestra. Because the violins are marked "*animato*," some conductors, notably Günter Wand, increase the tempo at this point—an exciting effect when well-managed.

2. Transition: This consists of the alphorn theme speeded up, played by flute followed by French horn.

3. Second Subject: A lyrical song for violins over a repeated bass line ("ground bass") suggested by the descending phrase that opened the movement, followed by a plaintive strain for oboe, leading to...

4. Swirling strings introduce an expanded version of the leaping theme from the introduction (the one we heard just before the sudden crash the introduced the alphorn melody), leading to...

5. A bold "college fight song" type tune based on the same dotted rhythm (dum, dadum, dadum, etc.) that

we heard in both the first and second movements, accompanied by festive triplets in the woodwinds and horns. This reaches a rousing climax and then immediately subsides to reintroduce the Big Tune.

The reprise of the Big Tune is not literal, however. Though more richly scored than on its first appearance, it veers off sharply into mournful minor keys and a reminder of the creepy pizzicato passage from the introduction. Brahms banishes this specter by leaping directly into the *animato* orchestral tutti, initiating a strenuous development section largely based on various bits of the Big Tune. This quickly rises to the most energetic single climax in the entire symphony: an angry, violent fist-shaking that sounds completely new, but actually turns out to be a variation of the alphorn theme. A full pause, then a huge explosive chord leads to the actual tune in question, bolder and more radiant than ever as intoned once again by the French horn.

As we heard in the first movement, the recapitulation of the second subject receives very regular treatment, its restatement in and around the home key of C major restoring tonal stability and anchoring the music once and for all. So as expected, the college fight song brings the second subject to a close, and a misty transition leads to the coda, with cellos, basses, contrabassoon, and bass trombone [nice if we get to hear the latter, as Jochum (EMI) permits] ponderously fixated on the first few notes of the Big Tune. There's another famous precedent for this "ground bass" method of introducing a coda: the first movements of Beethoven Seventh and Ninth Symphonies (and the finale of the former) use the technique as well. It imparts an unmatchable feeling of solidity.

Brahms builds a gigantic crescendo on top of his ground bass, and as he does the tempo increases and the first four notes of the Big Tune in diminution (shorter note values) provide the rhythmic accompaniment to pairs of musical exclamation points from the entire woodwind and brass sections. As the accompaniment (or *ostinato*) rises through the orchestra, the brass and strings cut in with a fortissimo statement of that soft, distant chorale that marked the entrance of the trombones toward the end of the introduction. This, then, has been our goal all along, timidly suggested, and now finally, blazingly asserted.

The chorale is very beautifully scored as it stands, but this doesn't stop many conductors from adding timpani for extra weight. I think this is a mistake; the brighter, more luminous timbre of Brahms' original idea strikes me as far more convincing. He may have his problems "writing loud," but surely not here. Having finally arrived at its goal, the orchestra then indulges in a few bars of grand celebration before the Big Tune's ostinato, now high in the violins, leads the dash to the victorious closing bars.

So how successful is this finale, not just by itself but as an appropriate ending to the whole symphony? There's no question that Brahms has crafted an amazingly well-balanced movement, formally speaking. For example, the point of recapitulation occurs at its exact center, usually just past eight minutes out of a total length of between sixteen and seventeen. But consider also that a finale that has no large repeats lasts as long as the entire opening movement—longer if (as is usually the case) the first movement's exposition repeat is omitted—and this despite the fact that there is no formal development section. The extended length is the natural result of there being so much thematic material, its sequential presentation, and perhaps Brahms' understanding that the inevitable triumphant conclusion must not be won too easily. Ultimately, the answer to the question of whether the struggle has been worth all the time that it takes depends on the skill of the interpreters as much as on each listener's subjective impressions.

In concluding this discussion of the first symphony, I want to share with you a wonderfully intriguing piece of current speculative scholarship. It's usually asserted that the resemblance of the Big Tune to the "Ode to Joy" in Beethoven's Ninth is intended as an act of homage. Some scholars take a different view, however, and see it as Brahms' corrective to Beethoven's introduction of voices and words into the otherwise abstract symphonic medium. In other words, by using an obviously similar tune in a purely instrumental context, Brahms "reclaims" the classical symphony. It's an interesting notion, and one that surely can't be discounted out of hand. Intentional or not, this is certainly the result that Brahms achieved.

Chapter 4

Symphony No. 2 in D Major, Op. 73 (1877)

IN HIS SECOND SYMPHONY, Brahms takes a major step toward reconciling the Romantic love of self-contained, beautiful melodies with the demands of large-scale form, and he does it in the most radical, indeed obsessive way possible. In the First Symphony, we saw that only the finale uses what might be called a genuine "song tune," the one singled out as resembling Beethoven's famous "Ode to Joy" from his Ninth Symphony. The form of Brahms' tune, in three phrases having the shape AAB, turns out to be significant, for every movement in the Second Symphony features a melody of this type, and the work's innate songfulness has made it arguably the most popular of all the symphonies.

Brahms, as has already been mentioned, put a very high value on melody, and was a huge admirer of popular and folk song. Like most great composers, he saw only two kinds of music, good and bad, and he enjoyed the good wherever he found it, without pretension or elitism. In constructing an entire symphony out of a particular type of tune, he was making the same kind of statement that his Romantic Nationalist colleagues Dvořák and Tchaikovsky were making with the folk music of their native countries, if perhaps inevitably with a less obviously ethnic slant. The AAB form that he chose to work with is one of the most common, universal, and simple melodic shapes in Western civilization. Consider the following well-known examples:

Elvis Pressley: "Hound Dog"
Verdi: *La donna e' mobile* from "Rigoletto"
Dvořák: Symphony No. 8: Allegretto grazioso (third movement)
The Beatles: "Hard Day's Night"
Tchaikovsky: Symphony No. 5: Andante cantabile (second movement horn solo)
Falla: *Canción del amor dolido* from "El amor brujo"
Rachmaninov: Rhapsody on a Theme of Paganini (18th variation)
Verdi: *Tacea la notte* from "Il trovatore"
Gershwin: Rhapsody in Blue (the lyrical "big tune")
Berlioz: Symphonie fantastique (the recurring "idée fixe")
Rogers and Hammerstein: "Oklahoma"

Some of the earlier examples are independent melodies, others occur in the context of larger forms, but all of them, without exception, are the tunes that you are most likely to remember, to come away humming, and the ones that contribute most to each piece's enduring popularity. This AAB structure also forms the basis for many other widely encountered melodic shapes, including AABB (frequent in the Classical period and the basis of most works in variation form), and AABA (ubiquitous in both classical and popular music alike, as we already saw in connection with Beethoven's "Ode to Joy" theme). The big advantage to AAB, and it's one that Brahms seizes with particular relish, is that it tends to be somewhat open-ended and so welcomes repetition and extension of its "B" part, a fact that aids musical continuity.

It's also useful to note that there are several different families of AAB tunes. For example, it is almost standard practice for the second "A" phrase to be varied slightly. In actual songs, the rhythm may change to accommodate the words, and it's even more common for the second phrase to be altered harmonically or melodically, with the basic rhythmic shape preserved, so as to set up the melody's continuation into "B." You will hear several examples of this in Brahms' Second, as also the expansion of "B" into one of those rich, yearning, lyrical climaxes so beloved of Romantic composers in general. This latter habit is a Russian specialty—the Rachmaninov cited earlier offers a particularly juicy example—but in the second subject of this symphony's first movement, Brahms proves himself to be no slouch in this department either.

Using similar melodic shapes in each movement constitutes a particularly helpful way to create a feeling of unity throughout the symphony. Musical ideas are not limited to actual tunes, and methods for binding multi-movement works together into a larger whole go well beyond the literal quotation or recall of earlier themes. Indeed, one of the most powerful (and infrequently discussed) binding techniques is not literal repetition, but rather suggestion—the ability to hint audibly at relationships between outwardly different melodies, producing what is in effect a "family" resemblance.

Haydn and Beethoven were both masters at this technique, and so was Brahms.

Working with self-contained melodies, or structurally similar families of melodies, has its risks. As suggested previously, really beautiful and distinctive tunes tend to resist being developed symphonically. This was one potential flaw in the First Symphony's finale, and the solution that Brahms presents here constitutes one of the Second Symphony's most striking and powerful expressive features. Perhaps even more dangerous is the possibility of rhythmic monotony, which undermines the momentum that symphonic movements, particularly quick ones, must have to fulfill their mandate as expressive journeys embodying "dramatic motion through time." To see one way in which Brahms tackled this issue, consider chart 1 showing time signatures for each movement in the four symphonies:

Symphony	No. 1			
Movement	1	2	3	4
Meter	6/8	3/4	2/4	4/4
Symphony	No. 2			
Movement	1	2	3	4
Meter	3/4	4/4-12/8	3/4-2/4-3/8	2/2
Symphony	No. 3			
Movement	1	2	3	4
Meter	6/4	4/4	3/8	2/2
Symphony	No. 4			
Movement	1	2	3	4
Meter	2/2	6/8	2/4	3/4

Chart 1   Time Signatures

A "time signature" simply tells us how many beats occur in each bar of music (the first or top number), and which note value equals one beat (the second or bottom number). As you can see, no two works have exactly the same metrical scheme, and all of them alternate movements in duple (2/2, 2/4, 4/4) with movements in triple (3/4, 3/8) meter. Time signatures that can be both duple and triple (6/4, 6/8, 12/8), depending on the accentuation within the bar, are called "compound" meters, and like triple meters they tend to have a more lilting rhythmic lift. Contrasts in meter prevent the music from becoming rhythmically stiff and tedious over long stretches. In discussing the First Symphony, we noted that the 6/8 "light" meter of the first movement gave it a propulsive character that helped greatly in sustaining its momentum. Similarly, the finale's 4/4 meter resulted in a somewhat foursquare solidity that counterbalanced the first movement's instability, but also asked for skillful handling on the part of the conductor to keep from turning into a dogged march.

In the three later symphonies, Brahms avoids any suggestion of rhythmic stiffness at least partly through his arrangement of time signatures. Furthermore, what chart 1 shows about each work's large-scale organization is also mirrored at much finer levels of detail, in the length of melodic phrases and the rhythmic combinations within each movement. With respect to the Second Symphony specifically, if this is the work where Brahms' use of so many similar melodic shapes risks dullness, you can see that this is also the piece with the most highly varied metrical scheme both within and between its movements. As a result, the melodies sing with all of their simple, natural beauty, but never stop the music dead in its tracks, or give the impression of one of those operatic potpourri overtures consisting of a bunch of hit tunes loosely stitched together.

Another telling rhythmic characteristic of the Second Symphony is the predominance of triple and compound time. As you can see, all of Brahms' symphonies feature two movements in duple meter and two in triple or compound meter. However the inner movements of the Second are special, in that duple and triple/compound meters freely intermingle and contrast with each other. The first movement—Brahms' longest, especially with its exposition repeat observed—is in 3/4, better known as waltz-tempo. Like the 6/8 opening of the First Symphony, this propels the music more forcefully, and also in this case more gracefully, than would a stiffer, more march-like duple meter. Only the finale employs an unambiguous duple meter, but with plenty of surprising rhythmic accentuation in its very quick tempo. So all of the symphony's AAB and other melodies find themselves in an extremely motion-friendly environment.

There's also one important touch of color that gives the Second Symphony's tunes a special character. Brahms omits the contrabassoon, and instead asks for a tuba—the only time one appears in his symphonies. The reason is quite clear: he needs the heavy brass instrument to provide a bottom to the soft, menacing trombone chorales at the start of the symphony. However, the practical effect of this decision is to lighten the sound of the woodwind choir generally, since the tuba lacks the gruff, wooly timbre of the contrabassoon and, being capable of playing louder, adds a touch of extra luster to the brass-laden climaxes of the outer movements. Small details such as this may not seem like much, but the contrasts created over forty-five–fifty minutes of playing time can leave a subtle and lasting impression.

First Movement: Allegro non troppo [not too quick]
Scoring: pairs of flutes, oboes, clarinets, bassoons, and trumpets; four horns; three trombones, tuba, timpani, and strings

It's entirely typical of Brahms that his sunniest symphony contains some of his darkest orchestral colors, in the form of the menacing trombones and tuba that intrude on the otherwise radiant opening. Indeed, the First and Second Symphonies belong together, a contrasting pair just like the Academic Festival and Tragic Overtures. There is in Brahms an almost compulsive need to "balance out" the expressive and formal elements of a given work by going immediately to the opposite pole in the next one. As you can see, this yin-and-yang tendency operates on both the large and small scales, and in many different ways. Accordingly, if the monothematic opening movement of the First Symphony represents Brahms' at his most melodically economical, the corresponding part of the Second Symphony features the most tunefully rich and diverse music in all of his works in the medium.

The melodic effusiveness of this first movement operates both vertically and horizontally; that is, there are a lot of tunes presented sequentially, but also contrapuntally combined simultaneously. The very first measures offer a perfect illustration of this. Cellos and basses begin the symphony with a three-note lead-in that sounds as if they want to play Stephen Foster's "Beautiful Dreamer," only to be interrupted immediately by a new idea on horns and bassoons answered by clarinets and flutes. But if you listen carefully, you will note that the melody on the lower strings doesn't stop. It continues below in its own, unruffled way. So although the music is basically quiet, there's actually quite a bit happening, and this in turn establishes a latent tension that Brahms will exploit very effectively as the movement proceeds.

Although I introduced the discussion of this symphony by focusing on tunes having an AAB phrase-structure, Brahms uses other melodic archetypes as well. The upper melody on horns and winds, for example, is a "question and answer" tune of a kind made famous in the finale of Mozart's Symphony No. 40 in G minor. Other examples include the first subject in the opening movement of Dvořák's "New World" Symphony, or the folk song "Green Grow the Rushes, O" when performed in call-and-response style, by one singer followed by a larger group. This easygoing dialog meanders to a gradual halt as timpani, trombones, and tuba intone their soft chorale. As I mentioned previously, this is the only Brahms symphony that requires the tuba, typically introduced right away so as to establish its presence as an active participant in the ongoing discourse.

The alternation of low brass and high woodwinds timidly sounding the symphony's three-note lead-in echoes the same "question and answer" shape of the melody we just heard, but before this ominous passage has much time to register the sun comes out from behind the clouds in the form of a gorgeous new melody for violins answered by the flute, and then joined by full strings and woodwinds. A swift crescendo brings us back to a forte counterstatement of "Beautiful Dreamer" for the full orchestra (minus low brass and timpani). I have always found this climax to be somewhat clunky-sounding, a textbook instance of Brahms' occasional discomfort in "writing loud," but with careful handling of the horns and trumpets, as we get from Jochum (EMI) or Giulini/Los Angeles (DG), the passage can sound full but not cramped.

This brief outburst, which effects an energetic transition to the second subject, vanishes as rapidly as it arrived, lighthearted staccato woodwinds making a rapid diminuendo. Looking back on this entire complex of ideas constituting the movement's "first subject," we note that it has two parts with an interruption (low brass and timpani) between them. The second subject has a similar shape, though its melodic ideas are even broader and more lyrical. First comes a tune very close in sound to Brahms' famous lullaby, given here to the violas and cellos and marked "singing" (*cantando*). It has a classic AAB form, with the second "A" repeated a bit higher to increase its yearning intensity, and "B" rising to an expansive and typically Romantic climax. Brahms then starts to repeat the tune, but instead the strings and woodwinds carry the melody upward in rising sequences, gaining in volume until a new, jagged idea for full orchestra (without timpani) interrupts the process.

Once again we see a typically Brahmsian duality: the first subject's "interruption" was quiet and solemn. This one is loud and agitated. Brahms marks it *"quasi ritenente,"* which means "as if holding back," the point being to allow sufficient time to make the jagged rhythms really speak, but it's very important that conductors observe the "as if" caution. When they don't the music tends to take on a stiff, exaggeratedly jerky quality that undercuts the momentum that Brahms is trying to maintain going into the next section—a very beautiful, sweeping melody for upper and lower strings in canon (i.e., one part following the other, as in a round), against a throbbing, syncopated accompaniment that actually starts a bit earlier, breaking in on the previous episode. The shape of this idea is also AAB, though in this case "A" is expansive and "B" is a brief cadence in descending scales only four bars long.

Some commentators view this exposition less as having two big halves, than as falling into three sections: the opening complex, the lullaby, and the canonic theme. This kind of shape follows a pattern found in Schubert's "Unfinished" and "Great" Symphonies, which Brahms knew and loved. Either view offers an equally valid description of the audible facts, and it really doesn't matter which one we adopt. What is more interesting, to my mind, is the way that Brahms unifies such a thematically generous exposition as a whole. For example, the canonic melody clearly derives from the woodwinds' "answer" in the symphony's opening idea. Also, the exposition closes with a return of the lullaby in the second violins and violas, followed by flutes and oboes. The result gives the impression of a huge but undeniably integrated musical statement.

The lullaby slowly dissolves into recollections of the symphony's opening bars, and at this point conductors have the option of continuing on to the development section or repeating the exposition. As this is Brahms' longest symphonic first movement, most choose to omit the repeat, particularly in live performances. On recordings the repeat gets observed slightly more frequently (the Jochum and Giulini performances previously mentioned take it, though both conductors also made recordings without), but the vast majority traditionally dispense with it all the same.

Unlike the similar point in the First Symphony, which tends to sound artificially abrupt and perhaps a touch dutiful rather than necessary, Brahms has prepared this particular lead-back extremely well. I feel personally that the exposition has so much material that it benefits the listener to hear it all again before moving on. If the basic tempos are well chosen, the repeat certainly doesn't make the piece sound longer—just the opposite in fact. It also has the effect of telling us exactly where the exposition ends and the development begins, and this in turn allows us better to prepare ourselves to follow some of the most intricate, tempestuous, and expressively affecting music that Brahms wrote.

It's also some of the most compressed. With the repeat, the exposition lasts about nine or ten minutes. The development section only takes about two or three, but it's a wild ride while it lasts. Remember I mentioned that the problem with writing Big Tunes is that we don't want to hear them "developed," merely repeated in all of their pristine beauty. Brahms takes this advice to heart, and ignores the entire second subject, which is where the exposition's most fully fledged melodies reside. The first subject, on the other hand, consisted of a large variety of distinctive motives, and all of them feature prominently in the drama that follows. It begins with a return to the horn's initial statement from the symphony's opening, followed immediately by an important new idea on solo oboe and second violins (where the original woodwind's "answer" would have been) formed out of the three-note motive for lower strings that launched the movement.

Flutes repeat the horn's theme, followed by the rest of the woodwinds with a spiky, staccato version of the oboe's newly minted answer. This gets the strings going and the energy level rises, generating what's called a "fugato," or a passage in counterpoint that imitates the first part (also called an "exposition") of a fugue, in which the main theme (or subject) is presented sequentially in all of the parts. The subject of this particular fugato is the original woodwind "answer" that Brahms just replaced with his new idea for solo oboe. It has the effect of a strenuous discussion, or argument. Taken up section by section in the strings, with plenty of commentary from the woodwinds, the fugato runs smack into the trombones and tuba, who spit out the symphony's opening motive in really angry, dissonant harmony.

Brahms has made an expressive virtue of the fact that any kind of development of extremely beautiful thematic material is going to make it sound, well, less beautiful. Here it turns downright ugly, and the remainder of the development can be described in very graphic terms as a violent reaction against this outbreak of hostility. The strings shudder, and attempt to "run away" using the first subject's energetic transitional material. With the addition of a forte roll on the timpani (for the first time in this development section), the brass and woodwinds proclaim in sequence the first two notes of the opening horn theme, answered by (a) the woodwinds with a version of the lovely violin melody that originally followed the dark chorale for trombones and tuba, and (b) the new idea based on the symphony's opening.

It takes two more varied repetitions of this complex of ideas before the music finally settles down and eases into the recapitulation. Readers interested in a little musical detective-work might find it interesting to compare the earlier passage with a remarkably similar section—conceptually, not melodically—from the first movement development of

Dvořák's Third Symphony of 1872 (from rehearsal letter E, measure 168), a work that Brahms, and very few others at the time, actually knew. Dvořák submitted the piece as part of his application for an Austrian state grant, and Brahms was a member of the jury. Coincidence? Unconscious reminiscence? There's no way to say for certain, and it really doesn't matter save as a further reminder of how much we don't know about the nineteenth century's most intriguing musical friendship.

This development section is also noteworthy for revealing a very important point about what "development" means. You may hear commentators saying that in most development sections the main thematic material is "broken up," "fragmented," or otherwise disassembled in some way. Here, just the opposite happens. The symphony's three-note opening motive becomes an extended phrase; the fugato takes a short idea and turns it into a strenuous discussion. Drama occurs as this vigorous attempt at growth and expansion turns nasty, and ultimately gets derailed by the violent interruptions of the opening horn motive. So don't assume that a composer must always hack his material to bits in a given development section. Particularly in this case, Brahms creates energy and builds his climaxes by enhancing the music's continuity and focusing on just a few ideas from the exposition.

The recapitulation opens with the original horn theme given to the oboes, and the woodwind "answer" now in the second violins and violas. First violins add a filigree counterpoint in quiet eighth notes—like tiny rivulets of sweat after an unexpectedly strenuous bout of physical activity. Because the first subject occupied the development section exclusively, Brahms cuts it down to its bare essence here: an extended dying fall for flute and oboe over softly murmuring strings, and the dark chorale at first represented only by two pianissimo timpani rolls. The third timpani roll wakes up the trombones and tuba, but their contribution now sounds more quizzical then menacing. Brahms then cuts directly to a more richly scored second subject that, as in the First Symphony, appears in its entirety for the same reasons stated in that discussion.

A last reminder of the symphony's opening, for woodwinds and trumpets over a long timpani roll, then introduces one of Brahms' longest and most poetic codas. Like the development section it's based entirely on the first subject—yet another reason why Brahms cut it short in the recapitulation. First, a nostalgic meditation for solo horn and strings leads to the initial horn theme being turned into an AAB-type melody on the violins. The effect is to purge all memory of the development section's nastiness. This is immediately varied, and then the woodwinds begin to dance lightly, over pizzicato strings. In this utterly carefree atmosphere, the movement draws to a gentle close with even trombones, tuba, and timpani contributing to the contented final chord.

Second Movement: Adagio non troppo
[Slowly, but not too much]
Scoring: Same as first movement, but only two horns

As you can see from the tempo designations both for this movement and several others, Brahms is the musical king of "*non troppo*," or "not too much," as well as "*poco*" or "a little bit." The trap for conductors is that all of these qualifiers, which apply to dynamics as much as tempo and phrasing, impose on the music a certain bland sameness when

Brahms is only trying to emphasize the importance of clear phrasing and clean rhythm. This adagio, one of Brahms' most original and harmonically expressive pieces, offers a case in point. Its opening theme for cellos, another one of the symphony's AAB tunes, is an exercise in ambiguity, from the cloudy harmony of its first two phrases, darkened by trombones and tuba, to the solemn continuation that charts a remarkable and totally unpredictable melodic course before returning to a simplified statement of the basic AAB theme.

Brahms' phrasing here is as free as his harmony, with the rhythm flowing across the bar lines of the basic 4/4 meter. I'm not a fan of counting while music is playing, but this is a case where you really can hear the music's unique rhythmic character if you do it properly. The movement, and the melody, actually begins on an upbeat—that is, on the fourth beat of the measure (or bar); so if you start counting the four quarter notes to each bar with "one" on the *second* note that you hear, and "two" on the *third* note, you'll be in the correct tempo and in the right rhythm to hear just how unusual the phrasing of this tune really is. I make a point of this because, especially in slow tempos, creating and sustaining momentum is a major priority in terms of the sonata style, and rhythmic displacement offers an important way to do it.

Both in terms of sound and harmonic coloration, this idea had a huge influence on British composer Edward Elgar, whose most characteristic descriptor, "*nobilmente*" ("nobly"), perfectly captures the music's gravity and dignity. By itself, this initial melody lasts sixteen bars, and represents the first part of a sonata form first subject. The second part is another fugato that takes the first two notes of "B" as its starting point. It's a very strange idea, hovering over a narrow range of notes and just as harmonically "naked" as the first theme was rich. The instruments enter in this order: horn, oboes, flutes, and lower strings. As if to highlight the relationship, "B" actually returns after the last entrance of the fugato subject in cellos and basses, rounding off the first subject in the violins.

For the second subject, the meter changes to 12/8, which is actually the same as 4/4 in terms of how it's counted—it's just that the basic unit of rhythm becomes an eighth note, and three of them equal one quarter note of the previous tempo. "The same tempo," Brahms writes, "*ma grazioso*." I won't ask you to count this new melody, which also begins on an upbeat and remains syncopated throughout. It's thoroughly charming, starting daintily in the flutes and oboes, before moving to the clarinets, oboes, and bassoons, and finally the strings. As soon as the violins get a hold of it the harmony darkens, passion increases, and the music quickly reaches a climax, followed by a warm closing theme for the strings eventually joined by the woodwinds.

Actually, this closing theme doesn't really close; it starts building to another climax that spills over into the brief development section. This takes the closing theme to a whole new level of emotional intensity. Trombones interrupt with a series of painful groans (compare their similar role in the first movement development section), and the first subject tries to return, unsuccessfully in the violins. Once again the trombones intervene, and now the oboe has the opening melody. This time the reaction is less fierce. Flute and oboe try the first subject yet again, but the actual moment of recapitulation occurs a bar later, as the violins give out an ornamental version of the theme reshaped into the triplet (12/8) rhythm of the second subject. You can tell where you are definitively when you hear the "B" phrase and its continuation, more or less as it originally appeared.

We have seen that Brahms tends to compress his first subject recapitulations, and this one is no exception, even though it did not feature in the development section. As already noted, the fugato begins with the same first two notes as "B." So instead of rounding out the melody as previously, AAB, and giving us the full fugato ending with "B," Brahms cuts directly to the fugato as a sort of "B" substitute. As if outraged by the fugato's presumption, "B" itself then arrives in high dudgeon on the second violins (it's not easy to hear over the roiling first violins and the heavy accompaniment from the rest of the strings, brass, and woodwinds). This storm passes in just six bars, and comes to a complete stop. Brahms represents the entire second subject by its closing theme, phrased in a wonderful series of hairpin (<>) crescendos in the timpani, bassoons, horns, and strings. One last climax, and the movement subsides to echoes of its opening theme scored for flute and oboe, then strings. The poetic soft timpani strokes underpinning the last measures should be familiar to us now as a characteristically Brahmsian fingerprint.

This movement leaves a very emotionally ambivalent impression: at times solemn, wistful, delicate, and angry. It's music that needs time to sink in and become familiar. Contemporary audiences found the opening theme particularly puzzling, but once internalized, you may well find it unforgettable. Indeed, even before I got to know the symphony at all well this was the music that came to mind whenever I thought about the piece.

> **Third Movement:** Allegretto grazioso
> (Quasi Andantino) [Graciously quick-ish, as if
> a little bit quicker than regular walking tempo]
> **Scoring:** full woodwinds, strings, and three horns

Tempo designations sound so much nicer in Italian, don't they? This, one of Brahms' most delectable movements, is also one of his most sophisticated, and the best thing about it is that so many of its subtleties are perfectly audible and recognizable on initial acquaintance. Like the similar movement in the First Symphony, this one begins with a woodwind tune over pizzicato strings, in this case scored for a "wind serenade" combination of oboe, clarinets, and bassoons. I hope unsurprisingly by now, the shape of this enchanting theme is AAB. This is particularly easy to hear as "A" has only four notes (three if you don't count the little ornament on its third note). The extensive continuation makes as if to wander away from its straight and narrow harmonic path, but Brahms stops it dead in its tracks before returning to the opening, now modified to form a gentle cadence. This is the entire thematic substance of the movement.

Suddenly the meter changes from 3/4 to 2/4, and the tempo increases to *Presto ma non assai* ("Very fast but not excessively"). Brahms recasts the whole opening section that we have just heard in this new format. Dancing strings and gurgling woodwinds parcel out the music between them with plenty of unpredictable accents. A sudden crescendo leads to what sounds like a new theme for the violins and violas, but if you think about it for a moment you may recognize it as the "AA" bit of the opening melody played twice and inverted (upside down). The scampering games continue until the oboes and bassoon signal a return of the initial theme in its original form. This duly arrives on those instruments, harmonized differently.

This time around, the expected continuation moves in a new direction. The full string section carries the tune for a moment toward darker, minor keys, and the new melody that they construct out of motives taken from the theme's original "B" section comes very close to the opening of the Fourth Symphony's slow movement. Before this has a chance to sink in, the strings and woodwinds dash away once again, this time in 3/8, with a triple time version of the previous episode's second half (the bit with the inverted form of the theme), as if taking up the conversation in mid-sentence. Flutes, clarinets, and bassoons eventually signal the return to the opening, and after a big ritard it duly arrives, with the melody given to the violins, once again differently harmonized. Now, however, the original continuation appears complete, and the woodwinds take over the melody at its conclusion.

But this isn't quite the end. Violins, *molto dolce* ("very sweetly"), add a touch of solemnity in the form of a gorgeous harmonic digression, answered *espressivo* by the woodwinds with a chromatic sigh of pleasure, before bits of the theme's "A" phrase usher in the final bars. It's all over in about five-and-half minutes, but the impression the music makes is timeless. Some of Brahms' contemporaries found this movement too slight and lacking in substance for a symphony of this size, but I find it impossible to agree. Brahms seldom wrote

a movement so immediately engaging to both the mind and
the senses in equal measure.

Fourth Movement: Allegro con spirito [Quick,
with spirit]
Scoring: Full orchestra

Unlike the First Symphony, there's no "finale problem"
here. The Second Symphony follows the classical pattern
of putting its most complex movement first, and the issue
at this point doesn't concern writing a grand finale, but
involves finding the right one given what we have heard
so far. Tragedy, clearly, is out of the question, as is heroic
optimism. After all, nothing would sound sillier than a
victory over a struggle that hasn't happened. The Second
Symphony has its moments of darkness, and more than a
few of deep mystery, but these are passing shadows that only
add depth of contrast to its basically contented demeanor.
So Brahms pulls out all the stops and gives us the giddiest
music he ever wrote.

Formally this movement is a combination of sonata and
rondo forms. You may recall from the discussion of the First
Symphony that a rondo has the basic form ABACA. In other
words, the main theme returns between episodes based on
different material. This can be blended perfectly with sonata
form by simply repeating the main theme at some point in
the sonata structure in its home key, usually at the beginning
of the development section. The rest more or less takes care
of itself, formally speaking. Returning to the opening theme
in the middle of the movement "loosens up" the structure,
making it more episodic, and this tends to suit the comparatively relaxed ambiance of a typical classical finale even

when, as here, the thematic material itself is consistently exciting and surprising.

The movement begins with a wonderfully intense theme for all the strings, *piano* and *sotto voce* ("under the voice"). The intensity comes from having the entire section playing together quietly in a swift tempo, giving the impression of great power held in reserve. There's one other splendid detail: horns and trumpets gently touch in the first note only, like a brief flash of light. The instantly memorable sound of this passage undoubtedly inspired Dvořák at the opening of the finale of his Sixth Symphony, though the actual melodies and subsequent treatment are entirely different. Woodwinds soon join the strings, as the melody winds down to what sounds like a premature close. Pay particular attention to the woodwind entrance and the music that they play twice over (making four repetitions of the same little phrase, including the strings). You'll learn why shortly.

Suddenly, the full orchestra bursts in, apparently in mid-phrase, with a boisterous counterstatement of the main theme. The rest falls into the category of "making a joyful noise," a passage consisting of nothing but hustle and bustle as the orchestra tosses out rhythmic motives of various shapes and sizes. This cuts off as suddenly as it started (there are a lot of abrupt dynamic contrasts in this movement), leaving a solo clarinet hanging in midair. Flute, then oboe, give out a brief anticipation of the second subject, which now appears immediately on violins and violas. Brahms marks it *largamente* ("broadly"), which some conductors—happily not most—take to mean "slam on the brakes." Certainly some modification of tempo is required, but not so much as to halt the music's momentum entirely.

This second subject is the symphony's last AAB tune, and if you think it sounds a bit like the main theme of the third movement, you're probably right. Indeed, I wouldn't be surprised if some type of analysis shows all of the AAB themes in the symphony to be based on some shared underlying idea. Whatever the reason, be it shape of the melody or the way it's harmonized, it has a certain familiar, half-remembered quality about it, a characteristic that Brahms also exploited quite effectively in the finale of the First Symphony. After the strings have their go at it, the woodwinds repeat the tune and then the orchestra resumes its general celebration.

One more idea intervenes as part of the second subject, a sort of musical merry-go-round for woodwinds accompanied by pizzicato strings. Tovey traced this passage back to the similar idea in the finale of Haydn's Symphony No. 104, and if you have time might want to give that work a listen. The attribution makes audible sense. Once again the full orchestra storms in with a cadence theme, and a sudden diminuendo leads to the development section beginning, as just suggested, with a return to the opening melody, not quite as originally heard. The woodwinds keep interrupting, and this game keeps up into the development proper.

Once again the orchestra comes storming in, this time with a vigorous argument over the little phrase from the opening theme that marked the woodwind's entrance, and now you can see why Brahms and I asked you to pay attention to it. Charles Ives had a great time making fun of this passage at various points in his own Second Symphony, but it too breaks off sharply, as woodwinds and strings offer what sounds like a new theme in quietly rustling triplets. It's actually a variation of the opening melody, a fact that becomes clearer when the oboe has the original woodwind motive. The rustling triplets return and the harmony darkens mysteriously. Brahms gives out the woodwind phrase in long notes (augmented), a wonderfully twilit passage including soft trombones and tuba that probably inspired the opening idea of Mahler's First Symphony.

In this atmosphere of mystery, the first theme returns to initiate the recapitulation. Since we've heard the woodwind phrase about a million times by now, Brahms leaves it out here, instead varying and extending the melody until the expected orchestral eruption. This is hugely compressed: after just a few bars a big, juicy ritard (unmarked but just about everyone does it) leads to the second subject, more strong and confident then ever. And so we go on to the woodwind merry-go-round, the closing theme, and then dive right into the coda. This truly does offer an apotheosis of the entire symphony as a glorification of AAB-style melody.

First, the full wind band, led by the trombones and tuba, starts playing a sequence based on the opening measures of the second subject. Notice that these instruments, the "emissaries of evil" in the first two movements, now lead the celebration in their own, somewhat gnarly way. Then the second subject breaks out in the violins, leading to an impressive diminuendo in a startling minor key, driving the music all the way back to the rustling, triplet version of the opening theme from the development section. This mounts in a huge crescendo, with pounding timpani, until the full orchestra seizes the opening notes of the first subject and presents them in the shape of the second: AAB.

As the violins circle higher and higher (this is the "B" part), the tempo seems to get faster. Brahms doesn't ask for an accelerando here, but it's so natural and the music seems to want it so badly that many conductors do it anyway. Good ones (like Jochum, Mackerras, or Bruno Walter in his New York Philharmonic recording) don't let the ensemble spin out of control. When it does, the result can be one of the most ungodly messes in all of music. Descending scales in the brass give us the next AAB transformation: the merry-go-round tune, now scored for full orchestra with wicked pauses after each "A" phrase. Finally, Brahms provides the crowning apotheosis: the second subject blasted out by the brass, AAB, rising higher and higher (it's especially thrilling if you can hear the violins here, as Giulini/Los Angeles permits) and coming to rest on a gleeful shout by the trombones atop the orchestra's final chords.

This is it, folks, the most unbuttoned music that Brahms ever wrote. After the Second Symphony, his symphonic music becomes more introverted, more reflective, and also angrier, but no less beautiful. In his typically self-deprecating way, Brahms liked to emphasize the Second Symphony's gloomier aspects, and commentators love to quote his statements to this effect. I won't. They only get in the way of what your ears are telling you: that the ending of this symphony is one of unalloyed happiness. So let's enjoy it as it stands; the next two symphonies will offer plenty of opportunities to consider darker, more serious things.

Chapter 5

Symphony No. 3 in F Major, Op. 90 (1883)

THE THIRD SYMPHONY has earned a special place in the hearts of most Brahms lovers. It is his only symphony that ends quietly, and partly for this reason it is the least played today. This wasn't always the case. As Walter Frisch has pointed out,[1] in Brahms' own lifetime it was more popular than the First Symphony, whose turbulent first movement proved difficult for many contemporary listeners. The Third is also Brahms' most compact symphony, as well as the most difficult to conduct. More than a few famous Brahms conductors, including Toscanini and Furtwängler, have made a mess of it, or come dangerously close. Exactly why this should be the case remains something of a mystery, but it probably has to do with the very thick scoring of the outer movements, which is difficult to balance and render with a sufficiently clear rhythmic profile. The fact is that

---

1. See Walter Frisch, *Brahms: The Four Symphonies*. Yale University Press, 1996.

there's more going on in the music than you will ever hear, and this can drive some conductors crazy—with singularly strange results in terms of tempo and phrasing. More on this shortly.

The Third also stakes out new musical terrain. Having solved the "classical" problems of form, movement, and melodic development in the first two symphonies, Brahms now begins to cast a wider net, and absorb some contemporary stylistic trends. This is a very sensitive topic, as it involves the notion of "originality" even beyond the touchy questions of national style that bedeviled nineteenth- and much twentieth-century musical scholarship. Let me be dogmatic at this point and assert that in music it makes no difference who did something "first." All that matters is who did it best. There is probably no formal or technical innovation attributed to a great composer that can't be found in the work of a less great contemporary or predecessor. The difference is that no one cares about interesting points of detail in otherwise dull or incompetent work.

Brahms, as we have seen, only took inspiration from the best, so we have nothing to fear on that account. Nevertheless, when examining the "influence question" it's usual to view him as living in a chronological continuum of German composers starting with Bach and moving through Beethoven—in other words, the "three Bs" approach. Great artists, though, take their inspiration wherever they find it, without prejudice. Wagner fancied himself the most echt-German artist of all time, yet few composers owe more to foreign (and specifically French) models. It's no discredit to Brahms as an artist to take an unflinching look at his models. To limit him, as much of the literature does, by placing him in a hermetically sealed aesthetic box strikes me as a mistake that hardly does credit to his artistic range.

What does all of this have to do with the Third Symphony? Simply this: it is the most outward-looking of the four. Like all such gestures in Brahms, whether deliberate acts of homage or unconscious reminiscences, these references are exclusively musical in nature. The most obvious of them concerns the opening theme of the symphony, which comes straight out of the first movement of Schumann's own Third Symphony (the "Rhenish"), where it occurs quietly some three-quarters of the way through. The equally soft ending of the development section of Brahms' first movement makes this tribute to a dear friend and mentor particularly clear. So far, so good, and comparatively uncontroversial.

However, the Third Symphony owes a far deeper debt to another composer and close friend, Antonin Dvořák, and this *is* controversial, not just because it is unthinkable that a great German composer should owe a debt of any kind to a Czech (yes, nationalist prejudice ran, and sometimes still runs, that deep in musical scholarship), but because the nature of this debt concerns the one area in which Brahms theoretically ranks supreme among Romantic composers: form and large-scale musical architecture. The work in question that possibly served as inspiration to Brahms is Dvořák's Fifth Symphony, a major masterpiece that even now doesn't receive the attention that it deserves.

Brahms, however, knew the work, as well as several of its predecessors. All of them predate the completion of his own First Symphony. I have often wondered, given that Brahms regarded Dvořák as his only serious rival in orchestral and chamber music, if the example of Dvořák's early symphonies—steeped as they are in the stylistics of Beethoven—was one of the factors that prodded him to complete and release his own First after two decades of indecision. The friendship between the two men, finally beginning to be explored in the scholarly literature (mostly from the Dvořák side), has a parallel only in the equally fascinating relationship between Haydn and Mozart. Until recently, the question of musical influence was viewed as a one-way street, from Brahms to Dvořák, but the audible evidence suggests a much more complex and artistically fruitful symbiosis.

Indeed, the two men had a great deal in common, not just musically but also personally. Both came from basically happy, lower-middle-class homes. Both shared a great reverence for Beethoven, and both gave up early performing careers (Brahms on the piano, Dvořák on viola) to devote themselves exclusively to composition. But there were differences also. Brahms represented the end of the line for the German symphonic tradition, while Dvořák was one of two founders (Smetana was the other) of the Czech national school. He thus had one foot in the Austro-German classical tradition that both he and Brahms so admired, and the other planted with the modernists represented by such composers as Berlioz, Liszt, and Wagner. For Dvořák this entailed no inherent contradiction; for Brahms it was impossible, and his feelings for Dvořák's music naturally were warmest in those areas where the two remained aesthetically close.

Nevertheless, it's probably fair to say that Brahms was a bit obsessed by his younger colleague. He was amazed at Dvořák's gifts for melody and orchestration, less impressed by his handling of form and occasional compositional untidiness, but he promoted Dvořák's work ceaselessly, even to the point of proofreading for publication the orchestral works of the Czech composer's American period in the early 1890s. Dvořák's Seventh Symphony, his most "Brahmsian," was a direct response to the German composer's Third Symphony, while Brahms' Fourth in turn has features in common with Dvořák's Seventh. That Brahms retained his affection for Dvořák despite the nationalist ferment that poisoned so much in the arts at the end of the nineteenth century, not to mention his own intense German patriotism, stands as a genuine tribute to his qualities as both a man and a musician.

We have already encountered Dvořák's Fifth Symphony as an example of the difference between the two men in their handling of the orchestra. Given the fact that Brahms does not quote (or even allude to) any of Dvořák's thematic material, what evidence is there that the Fifth may have influenced Brahms' Third? Consider the following facts:

1. Key: both works are in F major. In itself this doesn't necessarily mean anything. Dvořák's Sixth Symphony is often said to resemble Brahms' Second merely on the basis of this one point (D major in that case), but when you consider that both symphonies start in the major and feature stormy finales in the minor (a very unusual tonal plan), then the relationship becomes more compelling. You will not find this design in any Beethoven or Schumann symphony, for example, though it does appear in Haydn's "Emperor" Quartet (which both composers would have known), as well as in Mendelssohn's "Italian" Symphony (but only as a purely picturesque, ethnic touch because the finale is a *saltarello*, a specific type of dance closely related to the tarantella). So

for all intents and purposes, if Dvořák can't be said to have invented this particular device, he certainly revived it in a uniquely compelling way, one that Brahms cannot have failed to notice.

2. Form: This is where things really get interesting, because as noted previously, Dvořák is never given credit for being as ingenious as Brahms in this department. But even if he wasn't quite as powerful a master of development sections— a claim impossible to evaluate independently of the melodic material that comprises each individual work—Dvořák was certainly more innovative in terms of large-scale architecture, and nowhere more so than in his Fifth Symphony. For example, he links together the slow movement and scherzo with a rhapsodic variation for cellos on the slow movement's initial theme. This connection highlights the fact that the central "B" sections of both movements (they use a simple ABA ternary form) are variations of the same basic idea.

Dvořák also opens his stormy finale with a free inversion (i.e., the upside-down form) of the andante's opening theme, and as the music turns decisively toward the home key of F major in the coda, he brings back a recollection of the symphony's opening bars in that key. This was a device that was to become a favorite of Bruckner's, but Dvořák's method, the gentle way in which the music of the first movement steals in and signals "We are home!" is far more organic in feeling and logical in terms of development. Again, it's the sort of thing that Brahms would have noted, and as you will see his own version of this idea, while identical in concept, is entirely different in sound and feeling. Dvořák's symphony concludes in triumph, Brahms' in autumnal calm.

Even more significant than Brahms' handling of the Third Symphony's ending is what happens in the middle. As with the Dvořák, there is some thematic sharing between movements, and once again the middle section, or second subject, of the slow movement provides the source. In Brahms' Third, a tune from slow second movement reappears in the finale (rather than in the scherzo, as with Dvořák), but get this: the opening themes of both the slow movement and finale, exactly as in the Dvořák, are also variations on a similar basic idea (note the identical rhythms of the first five notes). Taken in isolation these details may not amount to much, but add them up and the evidence starts to get really compelling.

3. Orchestration: Many composers, from the Classical Period onward, characterize specific works by emphasizing certain tone colors. Preeminent in this department was Mozart, who could create an unforgettable impression simply by having clarinets available to him in addition to oboes. Indeed, as previously noted, the most important orchestral section in creating personalized "signature" timbres is the woodwind. Dvořák was a master at writing for woodwinds (it has always been a Czech specialty) and Brahms certainly knew just how important mastering this element of his craft was. The Fifth Symphony exploits two instrumental timbres in a particularly characterful way: clarinets and cellos.

These are precisely the sounds the Brahms also emphasizes in the Third. The clarinets present the first movement's second subject (a moment that possibly finds a tribute in kind at the same point in Dvořák's Seventh), and feature unforgettably at the start of the Andante. Brahms gives the most famous tune in the entire symphony to the cellos at the start of the third movement, whose time signature (3/8) is identical to that of similarly cello-led opening of Dvorák's second movement. Even the tempos are basically the same: for all practical purposes Brahms' "poco allegretto" and Dvorák's "andante con moto" are interchangeable. There are some other points of correspondence between the two works, but hopefully by now you see the point. If you have time, why not spend eighty minutes or so comparing the two symphonies in close proximity? You can listen to both in less time than it takes to see a movie.

None of these resemblances in any way mitigates Brahms' originality; he takes his ideas from whatever source and realizes them in his own entirely personal way. We will never be able to fathom the compositional process with sufficient certainty to assert that he knowingly borrowed from Dvorák (or elsewhere), but Brahms was too self-conscious a composer for us willingly to discount all of the evidence. More to the point, music is full of affectionate tributes of this kind, a sort of private, nonverbal correspondence between composers. Understanding this free exchange of ideas doesn't just deepen our understanding of the music, it also illuminates the role that some very positive human qualities, like friendship, respect, and open-mindedness, play in the creation of even the most personal, distinctive, and aesthetically "pure" masterpieces.

> **First Movement:** Allegro con brio (Quick, with verve)
> **Scoring:** pairs of flutes, oboes, clarinets, bassoons, and
> trumpets, contrabassoon, four horns, three
> trombones, timpani, and strings

This shortest and most compact Brahms symphony also has his tersest first movement. Its comparative formal direct-ness is matched by a remarkably high level of energy, and, in the exposition, some of Brahms' densest and most intrac-table orchestration. As a result, this movement has been sub-ject to more strange manipulations of tempo and balance at the hands of conductors than any of its brethren in all of the Brahms symphonies. Ironically, the best way to handle it seems to be to play it more or less exactly as written and trust Brahms to let us hear what matters most at any given point. There's a certain interpretive hypocrisy in play with respect to this movement, if you couple the reverence that most con-ductors have for Brahms generally with their unwillingness to observe his specific markings accurately.

Famously bad performances include Stokowski (Everest), who is particularly demented in his handling of tempo, and Furtwängler (EMI), who reshapes the dynamics of the open-ing in order to turn its straightforward sequence of chords into a cosmic event. It's exciting while it lasts (about five seconds), and limp as a wet noodle thereafter. Even among less interventionist conductors, this opening gesture, three chords for horns, trumpets, and woodwinds leading to the "passionato" opening theme in the violins, usually gets played as a crescendo. Brahms marks each chord forte individually, thereby indicating that a crescendo is exactly what he does NOT want, for the simple reason that he reserves this effect for the movement's coda.

Brahms may not have been a master of flashy orchestration and timbral "special effects," but he was a genius at knowing how to use simple tools with originality and freshness. To the extent that the Third Symphony is "about" anything, musically speaking, it represents a reaffirmation of what you might call orchestral core values—the fullness of a forte, the power of a well-placed crescendo, rhythmic suppleness—and a joy in primary colors: the sound of violins, cellos, horns, and clarinets. Structurally speaking, and particularly in the first movement, the various sections are unusually clearly demarcated and well-contrasted. It's almost as if Brahms is daring us to look for "hidden depths" when in fact everything he wants to say is right there on the music's surface. Consequently, many conductors fall into the trap of searching for buried treasure while missing the abundant riches located in plain sight.

If the exposition of the First Symphony featured "motives" rather than clearly defined tunes, and that of the Second had a large fund of melodies of all shapes and sizes, then that of the Third is remarkable in its fundamental simplicity: first theme, transition, second theme, closing theme. That's it. The exposition's brevity demands that the repeat be observed, which is still all too infrequently the case [although even some "old school" conductors such as Otto Klemperer (EMI) realized its necessity here]. The transition back to the opening as well as the music's continuation into the development have been composed with the kind of care that also suggest that Brahms had observance of the repeat in mind. For now, though, let's consider the thematic material of the exposition more closely.

First of all, note the tempo designation: *allegro con brio*, with no "*poco*" or other qualifications—yet another clue to the music's no-nonsense attitude. The first three introductory chords (the last overlaps the start of the main theme) form a motto that recurs throughout the movement. Commentators

are fond of pointing out that the motto then becomes part of
the bass line to the ensuing violin tune, but this is impossible
to hear over the timpani rolls, trombone chords, and inner
parts for the strings. The first subject already bears a striking
resemblance to the opening of Schumann's Third Symphony
in its rhythmic shape. Brahms accompanies this passionate
theme with a syncopated figure on violas and cellos very
similar to that at the end of the Second Symphony's first
movement exposition, only here, again, it's almost impossible
to discern at the forte dynamic. So don't worry about it and
just listen to the tune.

The music calms down almost immediately, as the violins
and cellos continue with a very broad transition theme starting with four repeated notes. Only now does the syncopated
accompaniment figure, which persists for almost the entire
first subject, peep through now and then. This passage,
which looks so simple on paper, is extremely difficult to make
sound rhythmically clear, not just on account of the scoring,
but also because the combination of compound meter (6/4),
triplet decoration in the melodic lines, and the omnipresent
syncopated ostinato accompaniment can come off as sloppy
and haphazard unless the conductor makes the players really
articulate the music cleanly—even at low volume. Needless
to say this is just what Brahms wants, but so seldom gets.

Pay particular attention, after the violins play their transition theme, to the return of the three-note motto in the
winds. The possibility of its erupting in unpredictable places
and leading back to the opening theme is one of the principal sources of dramatic surprise in the movement. For now,
it introduces a counterstatement of the transition theme for
flute, clarinet and bassoons, and together the woodwinds

and strings bring the first subject to a complete stop, but one that Brahms carefully leaves open-ended so as to allow the music's momentum to carry it right into the second subject, which is in a clear triple time (9/4)—almost a waltz tempo. Clarinet and bassoon lead off, *mezza voce* ("half-voice") and *grazioso*, to a delicious pizzicato accompaniment on the lower strings. The music's rhythmic straightforwardness forms the greatest possible contrast to the first subject's somewhat gangly fluidity.

Oboes and violas repeat this very attractive, bucolic melody, and Brahms now extends it with a delightful continuation for flutes, oboes, bassoons, and pizzicato strings. The violins reply wistfully by turning the tune upside down (inverted), then the oboe reintroduces the opening motto yet again. Ignoring this hint at first, the orchestra makes as if to continue the waltz, but a quick crescendo leads to an abrupt transition in a series of two-note ricochets in the upper strings, then it's on to the closing theme: a series of rolling phrases for the woodwinds in even rhythm, immediately increasing in volume and underpinned by a jagged rising figure in the violins. The harmony darkens toward the minor as the exposition comes to a close in a state of high excitement.

The development section maintains the clarity of utterance that we have come to expect of this symphony. It consists of minor-key versions of the entire material of the exposition played in reverse order except for the closing theme we have just heard, which actually gets the whole process started. First the waltz returns, wonderfully urgent on forte violas and cellos (Brahms marks it *agitato*), with its phrases extended a couple of extra beats to increase the tension. When this has run its course, the opening motto reappears transformed into an elegiac, cantabile horn solo that naturally leads to the first theme, but very mysteriously, pianissimo, in bare octaves for strings and woodwinds. You may catch a touch of the contrabassoon's deep, dark timbre here, though it tends to get absorbed by the double basses.

This flat description of the order of events is accurate as far as it goes, but it can't begin to describe the curious intensity of the music itself, arising from a mixture of major and minor modes as well as the character of the melodies. It's really very simplistic to insist on the basic major = happy, minor = sad antithesis. One of the reasons that the shape of this movement is so clear-cut is because its emotional character is so ambiguous (in the good sense of having many meanings at once), and so bittersweet. Although nominally in F major, a "happy" key whose characteristic archetype is Beethoven's Sixth "Pastoral" Symphony, there are shadows everywhere, and stormy passion is never far away. Brahms ensures that you always know exactly where you are so that you can take in the multifaceted melodic scenery all the more intently. If the themes never stray all that far from their origins, it's because their expressive potential is best realized by simple repetition rather than fragmentation.

For the moment, the orchestra has subsided in a state of mysterious calm. Suddenly the vigorous opening chords reappear, but take two attempts to actually launch the first subject once again. This recapitulation is quite different in shape from what we heard in the First and Second Symphonies. There, you may recall, the first subject was extensively abbreviated because it featured so prominently in the development section. Here, on the other hand, Brahms exploits the

second subject extensively, and uses just the first subject's initial phrase only at the very end by way of transition. So now
it reappears essentially complete, with a few nips and tucks
along the way. You can hear the most substantial differences
in the bridge passage to the second subject, which has to be
rewritten to stay in the home key of F major.

You might assume, at this point, that Brahms would
shorten the second subject substantially, but he doesn't. It's
also given complete, save for the traditional omission of
the counterstatement (formerly for strings). Another reason he leaves the music more or less intact has to do with
its brevity. There's really very little room to trim. Look at
it this way: without exposition repeat, the entire movement
takes about ten minutes at the proper, lively tempo. Using
Bruno Walter's excellent second (stereo) recording with the
Columbia Symphony Orchestra as a benchmark, these ten
minutes break down as follows: exposition (three minutes);
development (two minutes and twenty seconds); recapitulation (two minutes and forty seconds); coda (two minutes).
This is really, really compact for a late Romantic symphony.

Also, as you can see, Brahms has room for a very substantial coda. Relatively speaking, it's nearly as long as the
development section, and it's based (you guessed it) entirely
on the first subject, thus explaining why it appears so briefly
in the actual development, and also why we want to hear the
full second subject between the start of the recapitulation
and the coda. This is where the crescendo finally occurs in
connection with the opening motto, and where the music
rises to its angriest and most dissonant climax, before calm-
ing down to one last, crescendo-led appearance of the three-
note motto and a final, tranquil sigh in the form of the first

subject's initial phrase (a fleeting memory of Schumann, perhaps).

Second Movement: Andante [walking tempo]
Scoring: Full orchestra minus 2 horns, contrabassoon,
and timpani

The presence of trombones in the otherwise slightly reduced orchestration of this movement tells us right away that this movement will strike that special note of solemnity that invariably characterizes Brahms' use of those instruments. Together with the almost seraphic purity of its other principal ideas, this andante displays a spiritual radiance unique in Brahms' orchestral output, though the religious frame of reference isn't as unusual as you might at first think. For example, Brahms conceived the slow movement of his First Piano Concerto as a wordless setting of the *Benedictus* text from the Latin Mass ("Blessed are those who come in the name of the Lord"). There is no textual underpinning here that we're aware of, but the sacred atmosphere is, if anything, even more powerful than in the earlier concerto.

In keeping with the timbral color of the symphony generally, Brahms gives the main theme to solo clarinet, *espressivo*, accompanied by the second clarinet and bassoons, *semplice* ("simple"), all at the same *piano* dynamic. Examples such as this show that despite the claims of today's theoretical "authenticists," vibrato and a warm, vocal timbre were very much a part of orchestral performance, not just in the strings, but also in woodwind playing. In older music, *semplice* means "do not ornament the melody," whereas *espressivo* tells the player to highlight his line in relation to the others. Since adding notes ("ornamentation") or otherwise improvising on Brahms' theme is out of the question in this context, the soloist has only one recourse, which is to color the tune expressively, and this generally means adding a touch of additional vibrato.

Pay particular attention to the oscillating fragment of melody after the theme's fourth note. This will generate wonderful harmonic interest as this first section progresses. Once again Brahms chooses to shape a movement as "sonata form without development," though of course there's plenty of ongoing variation as the music proceeds, and so this description is as misleading as ever. The first subject takes shape as a dialog between woodwinds, stating the theme, and strings, which echo each phrase with more somber coloration. It may be that Brahms had the Adagio of Beethoven's Ninth in mind here, at least conceptually. There, the violins have the tune and woodwinds the echoes, but there's also a touch of melodic similarity as well.

After one full statement of the theme, Brahms immediately repeats it in a varied counterstatement with lovely ornamentation tossed back and forth from woodwinds to violins, the orchestra's confidence seeming to grow with the increasing dynamics. As the music quiets down, cellos and basses take over the theme and provide a transition to the second subject. This begins with one of the most radical passages that Brahms ever wrote: a sparsely scored, "spacey" idea for clarinet and bassoon starting with two repeated notes and continuing in rhythmically fluid triplets. The accompaniment consists largely of reiterations of those initial two repeated notes, first in all the strings, then with flutes softly added.

There are few if any precedents in earlier music for the fragmented scoring and harmonic ambiguity of this passage.

It looks forward to the timbral experiments of the Second Viennese School and the desolation of much twentieth-century music (Sibelius may have learned something from it too). This being Brahms, however, the mood lasts only so long, as strings take up a new theme in descending lines, with each phrase now echoed by the woodwinds in the exact opposite of the procedure we heard with the first subject. The space music returns, now only as accompaniment without the theme, and Brahms closes the second subject with a warm new melody for cellos and violas. This leads to what sounds like a development by the full orchestra of the first subject—or is it?

As the passion mounts, the climax cuts off suddenly, and a gentle transition for solo clarinet, flute, and bassoon (in that order) leads back to the first theme in its original shape, but with the orchestration greatly enriched. Trombones make their first, gentle entrance here and add a new warmth to Brahms' aural palette. Once the melody has run its course, another touch of development intervenes in the form of a lyrical extension for violins of the opening theme's first phrase. This rises to another heartfelt climax before subsiding into the strange second subject, greatly shortened and appearing once again as accompaniment only, without its melody. The scoring is even more ethereal, the harmony more elusive than before.

At the height of the mystery, the clarinet steals in with a wistful memory of the opening theme and so begins a brief coda, with horns and trombones prominent in the closing bars. Looking back on the movement, instead of "sonata without development" a more accurate description might be "sonata with interrupted developments," since the entire point of the structure is that drama (which is what development really means) tries to upset the music's ritual solemnity, but never succeeds. This is, in itself, a dramatic process. Indeed, there are few things in music more surprising than climaxes suddenly cut off, or appearing where you least expect them to be, and therein lies the genius of this astonishing piece. Its spiritual character is only deepened by its inclination to evolve in other directions.

Third Movement: Poco Allegretto [a little bit quick-ish]
Scoring: pairs of flutes, oboes, clarinets, bassoons, and horns; strings

This delectable intermezzo, containing one of the greatest melodies that Brahms ever penned, contributed hugely to the symphony's initial popularity. Indeed, it remains one of the best-known movements in all of Brahms, even though it appears in what is now his least frequently played symphony. Like everything in this work, the music's formal simplicity and melodic expressiveness mark it out as something special. The opening theme partakes of that "soulful minor" atmosphere—not tragic, but bittersweet rather—that we encountered in the first movement. It probably owes something to Brahms' experience with Hungarian and Slavic folk music. As initially presented, the tune represents the apotheosis of what an orchestral cello section can do in Romantic music, and like so many of Brahms' melodies when he is in "pop" mode (see the discussion of the Second Symphony), its phrases fall into the shape AAB.

That said, this movement is not without its pitfalls. Choosing the right tempo is critical here, as Brahms' own rather equivocal indication suggests. "A little bit quick-ish" can mean many things, but as a rule the more easily the music flows, the better. It's worth pointing out in this connection that the two benchmark performances by conductors of the old school (Walter and Klemperer), both raised in the living tradition of Brahms' performance, come in within one second of each other: 6'13" and 6'12", respectively. Seven minutes (Giulini, Bernstein, and Levine, all on DG) is pushing it, though the latter gets away with it thanks to his unsticky way with phrasing and rhythm. More than that (Eschenbach [Virgin Classics] at nearly eight minutes) and the music tends to sound more like Rachmaninov than Brahms, and in this context it becomes nearly intolerable.

Actually, the problem isn't so much the opening theme, which Brahms lets us hear three times: on cellos, violins, and woodwinds, with a gorgeous lyrical extension between the latter two occurrences, but rather the middle section, or trio. This is a dainty (no other word will do) tune for woodwinds in three-note sequences, answered graciously by the strings, the entire exchange occurring twice. As with the second subject of the Andante, the harmony here is a touch mysterious, the scoring extremely delicate. You simply can't emote all over it, and the melody really needs to move since one of its principal defining characteristics is its rhythm. And however similar it may be in tempo, this movement must form a contrast to the Andante that we just heard.

Once the trio has run its brief course, the marvelous opening melody returns in a famous passage for solo horn, then solo oboe. Bassoon and clarinet have the lyrical extension previously given to the violins, before those instruments have the final and most passionate repetition. This dissolves into a very short coda, with the music seemingly unwilling to let the magic end, but after one last sigh on the strings a gentle woodwind chord and a couple of soft pizzicatos bring the movement to its poetic but punctual conclusion.

Finale: Allegro [quick]
Scoring: full orchestra

This is a very physically exciting finale, at least up to the coda, and another movement in which choosing the right tempo is a critical factor in its success. The upper limit is about nine minutes, and closer to eight is even better, but absolute timings only tell part of the story because it's possible to slow down for the coda considerably while still delivering an aptly fiery allegro. Although very compact, like all of the movements in this symphony, Brahms also manages to make it the most comprehensive summation of the previous three movements in any of his symphonies to date, not just because he quotes themes from the earlier movements, but also because the music's character distills the essence of their expressive qualities and renders it in a particularly potent form.

The movements begins with one of Brahms' patented *sotto voce* string melodies—compare the start of the Second Symphony's last movement and you will hear an almost identical texture. But whereas the previous symphony's finale was all sunny geniality, this opening has the force of a gathering storm. As in the first movement, the sonata form structure Brahms employs here is almost schematic in its clarity and directness. The first subject has two distinct ideas: the menacing opening for strings based, as mentioned previously, on the Andante's first subject, and most remarkably, the same movement's spacey second subject that follows

immediately, transformed into a very dark chorale for clarinets, bassoons, and strings, with some gruff assistance from
the contrabassoon.

A sudden trombone crescendo initiates the swift and
violent transition to the second subject, a passage made of
jerky, two-note sequences that swiftly rises to a climax before
subsiding into the second subject. This is a heroic, major-
key melody for solo horn and cellos. The tune's pervasive
triplet rhythm may owe something to the preceding chorale,
and it's nice when the conductor lets us hear the chugging
string accompaniment clearly [Günter Wand's first recording
(RCA) is particularly well-balanced at this point]. Before this
has much chance to establish itself, the full orchestra comes
crashing in and wrenches the music back toward minor keys
with a closing theme whose rhythmic sequences hark back
to the trio section of the previous movement, though the
stormy emotional ambiance couldn't be more different.

Once more the orchestra rages to a climax, culminating in a virtuoso passage for violins with vicious *sforzando*
accents that some orchestras, most famously the Berlin
Philharmonic under Furtwängler (EMI), seem to have trou-
ble keeping together. Another volley of those violent, two-
note sequences, only this time with the first note accented
rather than the second, brings the exposition to a dramatic
close. Notice the pizzicatos in the strings as the music quiets
down, one of those Brahmsian fingerprints often in evidence
in transitional passages between major sections.

The development section that follows immediately is quite
short, and only uses the first subject. Brahms establishes a
mood of uneasy calm, restating the opening theme on flute,
clarinet, and bassoon, then on oboe and bassoon, alternating

with descending scales in woodwinds, then strings. As the dynamics reach pianissimo, the strings break the melody up into four-note bits. Some conductors evidently encourage the players to execute this passage near the instrument's bridge (in Italian "*sul ponticello*"), even though Brahms doesn't ask for this specific effect. It creates a wiry, metallic timbre that's quite appropriate to the threatening atmosphere Brahms evokes at this point.

It seems as if the music is going to expire in total silence, but suddenly the orchestra grabs hold of those four-note fragments of the first subject in a series of ricochets between horns on the one hand, and woodwinds backed by trumpets on the other. A sudden pause, and the chorale theme from the Andante enters in a canon between woodwinds, horns, and trumpets together, followed by the trombones, all set against a furious triplet whirlwind in the strings. If I had to pick one passage to illustrate Brahms' evocation of rage at its most vivid, it would be this one. Rising to a veritable paroxysm of fury, the entire wind section plus fortissimo timpani blast out the chorale theme triumphantly, in the major. Too many performances misjudge this climax, with mushy timpani and subdued brass. Brahms almost never writes fortissimo for timpani, trumpets, and trombones, and when he does, as here, he really means it. Excellent performances include Walter (Sony), Wand (RCA), Solti (Decca), Levine (RCA and DG), and Dohnanyi (Warner/Teldec).

The triumph, however, proves short-lived. Brahms now exploits a dramatic technique of which Mahler is the foremost master: the victorious climax "gone wrong." In the midst of jubilation, the harmony suddenly veers toward the minor and we're in the midst of the recapitulation, starting from its first jagged outburst. Compare this passage to the conceptually very similar moment in the first movement of Mahler's Third Symphony, at the climax of the "life" march on its initial appearance. Mahler admired this symphony, however dissimilar his aesthetic might have been from Brahms', and he certainly wasn't beyond learning a trick or two from his older colleague (the two composers respected each other and enjoyed a cordial personal relationship).

Brahms now follows one of his most powerful and effective bits of orchestration with one of his least. When this transitional passage first appeared in the exposition, it was a study in contrasts: sudden outbursts alternating with equally sudden moments of shadowed calm. Now he recomposes the entire paragraph to remain at an unvarying fortissimo, the opening theme still fragmented, but its four-note bits now turned into hard accents from the lower strings answered by the upper strings and woodwinds with the three remaining notes. It's a terribly difficult passage to play with the necessary force. Toscanini famously had timpani doubling the lower strings in one of his performances, with astonishingly vulgar and ineffective results. As with so many problems in this symphony, the issue is basically one of timing. If the conductor is playing the music quickly enough, the passage will have the ferocious impact that Brahms intends. Take it too slowly, though, and it simply sounds clumsy and rhythmically awkward.

As in the exposition, the music storms its way over to the second subject, which appears in full. So does the closing theme, although Brahms has another surprise in store when we get to its angular cadence (the phrase built out of two-note sequences): listen to the opening theme grinding below in the bass with almost hysterical force. It's a great moment in a symphony that has many of them. The recapitulation closes just as did the exposition, with three pizzicato chords, and the remaining couple of minutes are all coda, perhaps the most impressive and poetic one that Brahms ever wrote.

It begins, as did the development, with the opening theme, now phrased in the second subject's stream of triplets. The woodwinds take one last crack at it in something close to its original form, but the tempo relaxes (*poco sostenuto*—"a little sustained"—Brahms advises), as the oboe plays the tune's opening phrase in long notes (i.e., *augmented*) while the other woodwinds isolate just its initial four-note motive, which also happens to be that of the Andante's main theme as well. Simultaneously, the strings rustle tranquilly beneath, and if you listen carefully to the oboe, then horn, you might also catch the symphony's opening, three-note motto stealing in. But it's not quite the end.

Now the chorale enters, glowing in the soft and solemn colors of the full brass section. Brahms lets us hear it twice, the last time reaching a fulfilling *forte* before the opening motto returns yet again in the woodwinds, now finding its ultimate resolution in the peaceful return of the first movement's principal theme. The very last chord, typically, features the entire orchestra, including pianissimo timpani. Many commentators call the music of this coda "autumnal," others "nostalgic," and with good reason. It seems to embody the inimitable combination of contentment tinged with regret that characterizes so much of this symphony, and that seems to be its predestined final point of rest.

Let us take a moment to consider why this coda makes such a satisfying ending. As I suggested previously, it's not just the fact that it recalls the first movement's main theme. Actually, if you think about it, you will realize that what Brahms has done is to completely recompose, or recapitulate, not just the finale's exposition, but also its development section. The coda follows the course of the latter precisely, but removes all of its anxiety and tension, replacing those negative emotions with the spiritual calm of the Andante. And this in turn explains why Brahms bases his themes on those of the second movement: their final transformation is both something fresh and new—in terms of the finale—but emotionally familiar with reference to the symphony as a whole.

I began this discussion by citing Brahms' indebtedness to Dvorák's Fifth Symphony, but if you listen to the two, you will see that the similarities, while real, are in fact less important than the differences. This is how it usually is with masterpieces, and it's just as true in the other direction, the extent to which Dvorák sometimes resembles Brahms. The expressive ambience of this music, and its realization in formal terms, could have come from no one but Brahms, and there is nothing else like it in the whole of the Romantic Period.

Chapter 6

Symphony No. 4 in E Minor, Op. 98 (1885)

IN 1947 ARNOLD SCHOENBERG, the celebrated (and reviled) "destroyer of tonality" and subsequent inventor of twelve-tone, or "dodecaphonic" composition, penned one of his most famous essays, "Brahms the Progressive." In it, Schoenberg attempts to demonstrate, through a great deal of very abstruse musical analysis, that Brahms was not the backward-looking classicist of popular myth, but a composer with strikingly modern tendencies in many aspects of his compositional technique, particularly in his use of what Schoenberg called "developing variation." Although he doesn't define the term with anything like rigorous precision, what Schoenberg meant to describe, inasmuch as we can tell, was melody that progresses by an organic process in which each phrase generates a different yet related succeeding idea.

Schoenberg naturally had an ulterior motive. He was trying to prove that his twelve-tone method constituted the

natural next step in the evolution of German, and by extension, all classical music. His analyses are complex because
his own music is complex, written for "upper-class minds," as
he noted in his essay, and the more advanced he could make
Brahms look, the more plausible would be his claim to be the
latest link in the musical chain. Leaving all questions of self-
promotion aside, we can readily concede that Schoenberg
had a point. The continual harping on Brahms' obsession
with the past, on his formal conservatism and concern about
his place in history, neglects the very important fact that all
great musical works in established forms such as symphonies
necessarily reinterpret the past in light of the present, and
continually find new means of validating familiar proce-
dures. In short, they are inherently progressive.

This is particularly true of Brahms' Fourth Symphony, his
most advanced orchestral composition—music that plumbs
extremes of emotion from the jubilant to the tragic, and a
work that had an even bigger influence on twentieth-century
tonal composers than it did on Schoenberg and his fellow
members of the Second Viennese School (Berg and Webern).
That the symphony operates according to the principles of
"developing variation" becomes evident, in a basic sense,
when we observe that this is Brahms' first opening movement to omit the usual exposition repeat. Beethoven had
done it in his Ninth Symphony, as had Dvořák in his highly
experimental Third and more recent Seventh Symphonies.
Tchaikovsky and Bruckner also were freer in this respect
than the more classically oriented Brahms and Dvořák, but
for Brahms this was still a significant step along new paths.

The Fourth sports many other unusual features, starting
with its particularly vivid orchestration, including piccolo,

triangle, and three timpani (instead of the usual two). Its first movement is the only one in the symphonies to end loudly, indeed tragically, in a minor key. The slow movement has a bardic, almost descriptive quality that comes close to "program" or illustrative music. In the third movement, Brahms gives us a fiery new kind of scherzo instead of the brief, lyrical intermezzos in moderate tempo for reduced orchestra that feature in the three earlier works. But it's the finale that really gives the symphony its revolutionary character, one that explains both its comparatively slow acceptance in Brahms' lifetime as well as the high level of influence and esteem it has earned subsequently.

This finale, unique in the symphonic literature up to that time, is a *passacaglia*. As far as anyone can tell, the origins of the passacaglia go back to seventeenth-century Spain (*passacalle = passar calle*, literally, "to walk the street"), but since early notated sources come from Italy the Italian spelling has become the standard. By the mid-nineteenth century, the term had come to represent a set of free variations, often stately in character, over a repeated bass line (a "ground bass" or *basso ostinato*). Used in vocal music, the form became a favorite means of expressing grief or noble suffering, as in Dido's lament from Henry Purcell's opera *Dido and Aeneas*. Bach Passacaglia and Fugue in C minor, for organ, is the most famous instrumental example, along with his Chaconne[1] in D minor for solo violin.

It was Bach, in fact, who provided the proximate inspiration for the finale of Brahms' Fourth Symphony. As biographer Jan

---

1. Theorists argue about the technical differences between the Passacaglia and the Chaconne, but for all practical purposes the two may be considered interchangeable, particularly after the Baroque period.

Swafford notes, after making minor alterations to increase its harmonic interest, Brahms traced the theme of his passacaglia to Bach's Cantata No. 150, *Nach Dir, Herr; verlanget mich*. Here then is a perfect example of "Brahms the progressive." Passacaglias had been around for centuries, but until the Fourth Symphony's finale no one had ever considered the possibility of making a grand symphonic finale out of one.

The use of this supposedly "learned" and very ancient form gave the work a reputation for being particularly formidable intellectually, and even a bit one-dimensional emotionally (it's certainly obsessive—that's the whole point of a passacaglia in the first place). Later composers, though, immediately saw new expressive possibilities in the form, particularly as the level of harmonic dissonance increased and organizational principals other than the sonata style found increasing favor. Here is a short list of major instrumental works by important twentieth-century composers that employ passacaglia form, either by itself or as a movement within a larger whole:

Britten: Cello Symphony; Passacaglia from "Peter Grimes"
Shostakovich: Symphonies Nos 8 and 15; Violin Concerto No. 1; String Quartet No. 3
Walton: Symphony No. 2
Vaughan Williams: Symphony No. 5
Webern: Passacaglia, Op. 1
Martin: Passacaglia for Large Orchestra
Schnittke: Passacaglia for Large Orchestra
Hindemith: Symphony: Die Harmonie der Welt
Ravel: Piano Trio
Dutilleux: Symphony No. 1
Holst: First Suite in E-flat for Military Band
Schmidt: Chaconne in D minor

Stravinsky: Septet

It's probably only a small exaggeration to say that had Brahms not revived the orchestral passacaglia (his earlier and equally famous Haydn Variations also concludes with one), most if not all of the just mentioned works would not have been written as we now know them. Until the First World War, German composers set the standard for what was possible in large forms. Brahms knew it, and it may be that his sense of responsibility in this regard accounts for at least some of his inherent caution. Schoenberg knew it too, hence his anxiousness to be considered Brahms' legitimate successor (it didn't quite work out that way, but that's another story).

There's one final way in which Brahms' Fourth Symphony looks resolutely forward: it ends in the minor, with one of his most monumental fits of rage. It's a bit difficult for us today to understand just how radical a step this was. Between Haydn's *Sturm und Drang* ("Storm and Stress") period in the late 1760s/1770s, Mozart's two symphonies in G minor, and always excepting Mendelssohn's delightful but emotionally lightweight "Italian" Symphony, there are no important symphonies in the standard repertoire that end in tragic or anguished minor keys before Brahms' Fourth. Afterward, there are quite a few, including Tchaikovsky's Sixth "Pathetique," Mahler's Sixth "Tragic," Sibelius' Fourth, Vaughan Williams' Fourth, and Shostakovich's Eleventh. This is in addition to the entire atonal school, whose music for most listeners still represents a relentless glorification of suffering and misery.

In a very real sense, the expressive corollary to Schoenberg's emancipation of dissonance was the right of composers to value "truth" over "beauty," to wallow in despair, sorrow, self-pity, horror, and pain if they felt so inclined, thus denying their listeners the pleasure gained through music as a relaxing or entertaining leisure-time activity. Brahms would no doubt have been horrified at the lengths to which this kind of emotional self-indulgence eventually led; but the finale of the Fourth Symphony, and in particular its ending, surely played a part in making it possible. For this is no elegiac leave-taking, a resigned but sadly gracious farewell—not at all. Brahms concludes with a shout of defiance, a genuine "Stick that in your pipe and smoke it!" moment as disturbing, and as breathtakingly honest, as anything in nineteenth-century music.

First Movement: Allegro non troppo [not too quick]
Scoring: pairs of flutes, oboes, clarinets, bassoons,
and trumpets; four horns, timpani and strings

Up to this point in our discussions of the symphonies, we have stuck pretty closely to the language of sonata form: first subject, second subject, exposition, development, and recapitulation. In considering the first movement of the Fourth, I'd like to take a slightly different tack, at least as concerns the exposition, because although its shape is very clearly articulated in four sweeping sentences divided into the usual two subjects, these are also related to each other in several important ways and constitute an unusually unified whole.

The division into the two subject groups of a typical sonata exposition is a function of the composer's handling of harmony: you know you're in the second subject when the key has changed and this contrast persists for a long enough period of time. A change of key is usually accompanied by a new theme because melody and accompanying harmony together define the new tonality. However, the fact remains that most listeners, while sensitive to changes in key as manifested in the expressive qualities of the themes, do not think in terms of "first subject" and "second subject." We all simply take the music as it comes, as a linear sequence of events in time, and I've already noted that Romantic music generally tends to "thematicize" with distinctively lyrical melodic material points that, in the Classical period, would have been treated somewhat more mechanically.

In other words, transitional passages and cadence themes in Romantic music cease to be made up of obvious "motion music," designed to produce a clear feeling of going somewhere. This naturally entails a certain loss of momentum, one theoretically mitigated by the expressive character of the new melodies, these "motion music substitutes." The exposition of the Fourth Symphony offers a particularly cogent and masterful example of this uniquely Romantic process. The very opening of the symphony is less a tune in the traditional sense than a gently elegiac chain of two-note sequences, first on the violins, then followed by a counterstatement on the woodwinds. The most amazing thing about it is its feeling of latent power, of a destiny that already suggests the tragedy to come in the movement's coda. Just how Brahms achieves this quality can't be explained: it's just one of those things that music does in the hands of a master.

After the counterstatement, the violins extend the melody in a warmly songful passage that shows Brahms' rich-textured string scoring to particular advantage (very characteristic of the symphony as a whole). The violins seem headed for a cli-max as the volume increases, but oboes, clarinets, bassoons, and horns interrupt with an angular fanfare in triplet rhythm, answered by slashing chords from the full orchestra. Cellos answer *forte* with a new, vaguely exotic tune, accompanied by bits of the fanfare. These two ideas together, melody plus accompaniment, sound strangely like a tango, and the music has exactly that dance's darkly passionate character.

Technically this is the "motion music substitute," the tran-sition to the second subject. You might say that it achieves the necessary forward thrust on sheer personality alone, coming as it does after the more reflective, even meandering opening. Tchaikovsky was the grand master of the technique of creating lyrical melodies that really move, but it's a qual-ity that all of the great Romantic composers shared to some degree. Compare the wonderful suppleness and fluidity of Brahms' solution here to the somewhat clunky transitional counterstatement leading to the second subject in the first movement of the Second Symphony, and you can see clearly how far his technique has advanced in the decade or so sepa-rating the two works.

I'd like to expand on this last point a bit further, because it really is important for understanding not just Brahms, but the logistics of sonata form generally, and it shows that the problems involved aren't merely theoretical or aridly techni-cal, but common sense issues that all music lovers can appre-ciate and understand.

In the First and Third Symphonies, Brahms had less trou-ble creating forward progress for the simple reason that both expositions begin with driving, muscular, rhythmic themes. Starting with a bang, the music naturally wants to relax as it proceeds. The more lyrical secondary material offers an appropriate contrast of mood, color, and dynamics, effortlessly creating the additional characters required to populate the narrative to come. However, because the Second and Fourth Symphonies begin quietly and lyrically, Brahms must dramatize the progression from one theme or mood to the next, and this means providing some form of climax or energetic event, the reaction to which justifies the music's continuation. The alternative is either stasis, or a chain of disconnected episodes such as we often find in Bruckner's expositions (he found a different way around the problem).

It should be evident from the foregoing that the method employed in the First and Third Symphonies is the easier of the two. It was standard practice for Classical period first subjects to start energetically, but for some reason, possibly a result of their obsession with the mysterious opening of Beethoven's Ninth, Romantic composers often like to begin symphonies with the musical equivalent of a pre-dawn yawn and stretch. The difference between Brahms and so many of his colleagues simply lies in his grasp of this particular problem, and his determination to give his handling of form inevitability and life. The "tango" theme in the Fourth Symphony thus provides exactly what the music requires. It has rhythm, energy, and a character all its own without a hint of contrivance, amplifying and enriching what has come before while setting the stage for what follows. It represents a thoroughly Romantic solution to a Classical challenge, and is thus also modern and (to use Schoenberg's term) progressive.

The violins take up the tango theme only to run into a roadblock set up by repeated woodwind fanfares. This has the effect of knocking the music back to square one: a return of

the opening idea on pizzicato strings in dialog with woodwinds, its two-note sequences so familiar to us now from the
other, similarly scored passages already mentioned in the previous symphonies. The music now brightens into a major key
as a new, wholly sunny dialog begins, starting on the woodwinds and continuing with a gorgeously expansive answer
from the violins [listen to how unforgettably Marek Janowski
(PentaTone) handles this passage with the Pittsburgh
Symphony]. Technically this marks the start of the second
subject. All seems tranquil until a mysterious harmonic cloud
passes over the sunny landscape, with sighing strings and dis-
tantly calling trumpets over a soft timpani roll.

A new fanfare now takes shape for woodwinds and horns
in a triplet rhythm quite similar to the one that introduced
the tango. Another "cloud" passes by, and suddenly the fanfare erupts heroically in the full orchestra. Vividly tossed
back and forth between the strings, woodwinds, and brass,
this jubilant idea swiftly rises to a climax (note the off-beat
timpani strokes) only to be halted abruptly by yet another
return of the opening idea on woodwinds alone, now a calm-
ing influence, bringing the exposition to a close. I hope you
can see from the foregoing (and hear when you listen) that
although it may be divided into first and second subjects, the
constant return of the opening tune like a refrain between
sections, and the related fanfare ideas common to both
subjects, bind the whole exposition together into a single
sweeping paragraph phrased in four ample, well-contrasted
sentences.

The development section begins as if it were a repeat of the
exposition, but here, as noted in my introductory remarks,
Brahms omits the repeat and proceeds instead to the most

graphically eventful episode of its kind in any of the symphonies. He begins by letting the opening idea wander off in a new direction, its two-note basic motive extended to three on flutes and bassoons, harmonized sweetly in thirds. The full orchestra then takes up this new idea with brusque force, in a rough canon between upper and lower strings with woodwinds. A sudden crack on the timpani brings back the mysterious harmonic cloud that preceded the fanfare theme. This duly returns on flutes, clarinets, and bassoons in a variant so quizzical that you can practically see a question mark placed after it. The mystery deepens as the cloud passes from strings to woodwinds.

Suddenly the full orchestra breaks in with loud, dissonant fanfares, the harmony distinctly based on the quizzical variant just heard, seesawing between major and minor keys. Just as the minor seems to win the upper hand, the opening idea returns yet again, now in chains of calmly descending triplets mostly for clarinets and bassoons. The melody's second part, closer in shape to its original appearance, becomes more and more ethereal, at last dying out completely. Oboes, clarinets, and bassoons, *piano* and *dolce* ("sweetly") give out the opening idea in bare octaves, twice interrupted by the "cloud." Then Brahms picks up the tune in mid-phrase, as if nothing had happened, and we find ourselves squarely in the recapitulation, perhaps not quite sure how we got there.

Aside from omitting the woodwind countersubject, Brahms makes this recapitulation unusually regular, and with good reason. Both the tango melody and the woodwind/string dialog that opens the second subject were completely absent from the development section, so we need them to provide necessary contrast between the opening tune and the fanfare, both of which we've just heard extensively. You will recall that the latter idea wanted to head toward minor keys in the development. As if taking this into account, Brahms enriches its orchestration in the recapitulation, giving the music a bolder and even more resplendently triumphant cast.

Then something odd happens. The fanfare continues well past its original point of culmination, proceeding along lines very similar to what we heard in the development section. Technically this marks the start of the coda, but the music is so continuous that it seems pedantic to insist on a formal line of demarcation where Brahms has taken special pains to conceal it. You may notice as the fanfare struggles on in the strings and brass that the version the woodwinds are playing is actually the one that introduced the tango. All the movement's threads are starting to come together, and now the tragedy latent in so much of this movement's thematic material becomes manifest.

Once again the fanfare lands squarely in a minor key, and once again the opening theme answers, not consolingly in the major this time, but in the home key of E minor, whipping through the orchestra in a vicious canon between fortissimo horns and the rest of the orchestra. Each phrase of the melody becomes wilder and more urgent, until the violins reach a point at which they are practically screaming in pain. What makes this passage so powerfully tragic is the fact that we've heard it all before; the very literalness with which Brahms follows the course of the melody reveals the darkness lying at the heart of its original, windswept beauty. And once this becomes clear, Brahms drives home the point with a few devastating final chords punctuated by pounding solo timpani strokes.

To conclude this discussion of the first movement, it's worth considering two further points. First, having mentioned that Brahms often sounds uncomfortable "writing loud," this conclusion stands as one of the finest pieces of *tutti* orchestration he ever achieved. Consider only the fact that he manages this climactic paroxysm without even requiring trombones, and you'll immediately understand just how accurately judged his scoring is. Part of his secret lies in the fact that the music's intensity arises through playing the opening melody in its entirety, with violins dominating, rather than by sheer volume and density of sound. Second, it's common to refer to the Fourth as a tragic symphony, with specific reference to the passacaglia finale. Tragic it most certainly is, but for reasons to be considered in their place, the actual tragic events do not take place in the finale, but here, in the first movement.

Why does this distinction matter? Recall in our discussion of the First Symphony, I noted that the gentle, major-key resolution to the first movement created a problem for Brahms in explaining and justifying the return to previously explored territory at the beginning of the finale. Here, however, there's no issue because the tragic ending leaves behind an intense feeling of issues unsettled, a story not yet fully told. We naturally crave an emotional resolution to what we have just heard. The three remaining parts of the symphony can thus be seen as different reactions to the events unfolding in the first movement, and there's no question whatsoever about their aptness or necessity.

Second Movement: Andante moderato [moderate
walking tempo]
Scoring: Same as first movement

This is Brahms' longest symphonic slow movement, usually
equaling the eleven–twelve minutes of the opening *Allegro
non troppo*. The "moderate" qualification in its tempo designation encourages some conductors to take it too slowly; but
it's not an adagio, and the rhythmic cast of its themes tends
to encourage a more flowing treatment. Like every movement in this symphony, this one has important material
based on a fanfare. Announced at the outset by two horns,
bassoons, oboes, and flutes, this one bears a striking resemblance to the lead-back to the main theme in the Second
Symphony's third movement. Its shape is what I call a "mirror theme," because Brahms builds it out of repetitions of
rhythmic motives that are mirror images of each other: one
goes up, the other down (in this case).

A favorite melodic archetype of Dvořák as well, the lin-
eage of this kind of tune is very ancient, and it belongs in
the category of themes related to folk or popular idioms. In
the classical music world perhaps the most famous example is the fanfare opening of Haydn's 104th or "London"
Symphony, a work that Brahms certainly knew quite well.
The link to folk music becomes clearer in listening to the
main theme, a duet for clarinets accompanied by bassoons
and pizzicato strings, based on the same mirror motives as
the fanfare. It has a strongly bardic quality, a "once upon a
time" legendary mood thanks to its harmonic coloration.
Brahms subjects this very memorable tune to a series of simple variations (that for violins is particularly beautiful) that

further serve to confirm the music's picturesque narrative character.

Formally, this movement is one very familiar to us by now: sonata form without development section, which means that there's lots of development, only not where you expect it to be. In this case it mostly occurs in the recapitulation. As in the first movement, the transition to the second subject is a new theme in its own right, one with more energy than the main theme. It's a stern tune in steadily chugging trip-lets, announced *forte* by the woodwinds in alternation with the strings about three–three-and-a-half minutes in. It leads directly to a gorgeous, lyrical effusion for cellos, decorated by a rich counterpoint of violins. There's also an extended clos-ing theme, a graceful dialog between strings and woodwind (flute and clarinet), leading back to the recapitulation in which the main melody returns on divided violas—a won-derful, dusky sound.

It's worth noting that the recapitulation in most perfor-mances will occur at almost precisely the exact midpoint of the movement (in Carlos Kleiber's DG recording, it happens at 5'52" out of a totaling timing of 11'24"). After the horns take over the melody from the violas, instead of a series of variations Brahms gives us a sturdy, vigorous development of the initial fanfare motive for the full orchestra, and in doing so he reveals the true purpose of the transition theme. Where previously it might have sounded like an unexpect-edly sudden interruption of the first subject, here, backed by timpani, it makes a terrific climax to the strenuous develop-ment that we have just heard. It also revs up the tension for the movement's main event: the glorious return of the sec-ond subject on the full string section, sung out by the violins accompanied by the full orchestra (with timpani rolls)—perhaps Brahms' most effusively Tchaikovskian moment.

The coda returns hesitantly to the opening theme, at first on clarinets as originally, then *forte* for horns in a richly harmonized version of the opening fanfare. It's an absolutely magical passage, sounding an almost chivalrous note of farewell as the full orchestra comes together one last time for the *pianissimo* final chord. I said at the beginning of this discussion that this music is "picturesque," so much so that it almost begs a programmatic explanation. Is something going on "behind" the notes? It seems likely that after the tragic ending of the first movement, our first and most immediate reaction might be the need to escape into fantasy, or perhaps into an idealized past. Certainly this movement fulfills that desire perfectly.

As you can also see, this Andante is very easy to describe. You might think that its length makes it comparatively more complicated than its predecessors in the first three symphonies, but that's not the case. It is the size of the themes themselves that extends the timing of the movement, and Brahms achieves this in two very different ways. In the first subject, it is the repetition of small motives and their constant variation that creates bigness. With the second subject, it is simply the breadth of its lyricism, the most sweeping Romantic melody that Brahms ever put into one of his symphonic slow movements. The contrast between them is so great that the movement never feels its length.

Third Movement: Allegro giocoso ["cheerfully quick"]
Scoring: piccolo; flute; pairs of oboes, clarinets, bassoons, and trumpets; four horns, contrabassoon, three timpani, and strings

Everything about this movement is special. It is Brahms' first real symphonic scherzo, by which we mean a fast, muscular, dance-like movement similar to those in Beethoven's symphonies. However, instead of being in triple-time it's in a quick duple meter (2/4) because the preceding Andante moderato was in 6/8, and the passacaglia finale uses triple meter (3/4). This scherzo employs piccolo and triangle for the first time in the symphonies, and it also adopts three-drum timpani tuning that greatly increases the power of the climaxes (because more notes are available to reinforce them). Finally this dynamo of a piece, which was encored at the symphony's premiere, ignores the usual ABA scherzo-and-trio design, opting instead for full-blown sonata form.

The clue to its emotional character can be found in the tempo designation. Brahms does not often include emotional descriptors in his movement headings, at least not in the symphonies, but both here and in the finale he makes clear exactly the kind of expression he wants. So the music is "cheerful," but there's more to it than that. As a reaction to the tragedy of the first movement, this scherzo comes across as defiantly manic and driven, a determined attempt to be happy no matter what. Indeed, in describing the finale of his own Fourth Symphony to his patroness Nadezhda von Meck, Tchaikovsky put his finger on at least one very plausible interpretation of this movement's expressive point: "if you find no joy in yourself, go to the people.... there still is happiness, simple, naive happiness. Rejoice in the happiness of others—and you can still live."

Writing a quick movement in sonata form only six minutes long entails a good deal of thematic compression, and this only enhances the music's explosive character. This is particularly true with regard to the first subject, which contain no less than three distinct ideas arranged ABCBA, with "B" also serving as the transition to the second subject. Let's take a closer look at each of these elements:

A. The first thing to note about the movement's main theme is its unusual size, only five bars long. Tradition dictates that a *Luftpause* ("breathing pause") be inserted between the fourth and fifth bars, thereby isolating the *fortissimo*-accented "extra" low note to which the basic four-bar tune leads. "Old school" conductors such as Klemperer, Jochum, and Walter all do it to some degree, and it has the effect of turning Brahms' five-bar phrase into a clear 4 + 1, which strikes me as missing some of the point even if it adds a certain gruff humor to the opening (humor is never one of German Romantic music's strong suits, and it wasn't Brahms'). It also interrupts the music's momentum just when it's getting established. Interestingly, Hermann Abendroth, a conductor often associated with one of the most important and heavily interventionist schools of Brahms performance—that of the Meiningen Orchestra that premiered this very symphony—doesn't introduce a rhythmic hesitation at this point.

B. This is a simple figure in descending notes, repeated twice, in the rhythm "DAdadum, DAdadum, etc." Both the rhythm and the melodic shape (four notes in its basic outline) are very important, and Brahms finds all kinds of uses for them both together and separately as the movement proceeds.

C. You may find this motive vaguely familiar. It is a mirror-theme fanfare audibly related to the principal subject of the previous movement. British composer Gustav Holst may also have had it in mind when composing "Jupiter: The Bringer of Jollity" from his suite *The Planets.*

All of these motives are announced at full volume and high speed in a grand orchestral tutti, and it's a sign of just how pressurized the music will be that the entire presentation takes about sixteen seconds, on average. After we hear them for the first time, Brahms settles down to a more lyrical version of "B" before returning to "A" inverted (upside down), and bringing in the triangle. Like all special instruments in Brahms, once he decides to use it, he doesn't stint, and this triangle part remains one of the largest and most outstanding solos for an orchestral percussionist.

The second subject, introduced by the transitional version of "B," is a graceful theme on the violins decorated by jolly woodwind runs (note Brahms' happy use of the piccolo in a piano context here). Woodwinds and triangle then take up the tune in a perky, *staccato* variation, and this leads back immediately to the main theme and the beginning of the development section. This habit, of bringing the opening tune back at crucial points, also gives the movement a strong rondo feeling—it's similar to what we heard in the finale of the Second Symphony—loosening up the form and, particularly here, creating a more expansive impression than would otherwise be the case.

You're going to be amazed at this development section. It uses only the first subject, but because its ideas are so pithy, it finds room to discuss them in an amazingly varied number of ways. It falls into two main halves. The first of these, after some wild exchanges based on that extra fifth bar of the initial theme, focuses mainly on "B" and carries the harmony into the minor mode, but in a strenuous rather than unhappy way. This fades out to total silence, until with a tap on the triangle (a sly wink perhaps) the opening melody returns and introduces a marvelous lyrical transformation of the fanfare ("C") for horns, followed lazily by the woodwinds.

Suddenly the original version of the fanfare breaks out loudly in the full orchestra, and we're in the recapitulation. Compare this process to Brahms' similar technique of starting in mid-theme at the same point in the first movement. The rest of the recapitulation is almost literal until we get to what was formerly the perky woodwind counterstatement of the second subject, which is transformed into a galumphing march for full orchestra in triplet rhythm. The march storms onward, quickly reach a climax that's brought up short by a few sharp chords.

The coda then begins dramatically at low volume, with thrumming timpani in the rhythm of "B," over which the first theme peeks out of the woodwind section. A summons from the horns gathers all the forces together for one last onslaught, and the final minute or so consists of Brahms making the loudest and most brilliant sounds he knows how, with the fanfare theme "C" on the trumpets well to the fore, and the triangle jingling away with ferocious brilliance— even up to the very last note (remember Brahms' inviolable rule: all the instruments in a given movement participate in the final chord).

Finale: Allegro energico e passionato [energetically and passionately quick]
Scoring: full orchestra with trombones, minus piccolo and triangle

So far we've heard two very different reactions to the first movement's tragedy, and both of them might be classed as forms of emotional denial: a retreat to an idealized or mythical realm, and convulsive, perhaps somewhat forced, high spirits. But all tragedy, ultimately, is about the omnipotence of fate. So what better way could there be to bring us back to earth and describe fate's dominance musically than a passacaglia—a series of variations over an endlessly repeated bass line? Of course Brahms gives us more than that. This movement isn't so much a portrait of fate itself as it is an emotional attempt to come to terms with a singularly cold, hard reality. And so the music runs the gamut of feelings: despairing, pleading, accepting, challenging, and most of all, raging. At the end, it is rage that wins out while fate remains impassive and uncaring.

This impressionistic description might well be all you need in listening to this finale, and the truth is that few pieces of music speak for themselves more eloquently and graphically than Brahms manages here. However, there are so many wonderful musical details in this most innovative of symphonic movements that it's worth taking some time to point out the highlights. One word of caution before starting: you will not hear the passacaglia theme throughout the movement. When Brahms wants you to, you will. Otherwise, just listen to the melodic surface and don't worry about the rest. After all, if the music consisted of little more than a gazillion obvious repetitions of an eight-bar bass line, you'd be the one screaming wrathfully well before you reached the end.

The movement opens with yet another fanfare in the form of a boldly harmonized statement of the passacaglia theme (i.e., the recurring bass line), scored for the entire orchestral wind section, including trombones. Brahms is unusually kind to his listeners throughout this movement, "telling" us exactly what he proposes to do. And so in the first variation, against repeated timpani rolls and low notes from horns and trombones, the bass line actually becomes just that, in pizzicato strings. Then Brahms adds a lyrical woodwind counterpoint to the pizzicato bass line, followed immediately by a loud, sharply rhythmic variation for full orchestra. Throughout these initial stages the bass line remains distinctly audible, but moves gradually from foreground to background.

As the movement proceeds, you will notice that it falls naturally into larger sections grouped by similarities of mood, texture, or melody, with the bass line surfacing now and then as a kind of refrain separating the various parts. The first big section starts with the entrance of the bowed strings. Brahms gives them a striving melody that certainly lives up to the movement's "*passionato*" designation. This tune is varied several times, always with increasing urgency. In the last of these variations, wildly frantic violin figurations are twice interrupted by a "dying fall"—descending chromatic scales in the woodwinds. The passacaglia theme then returns, differently harmonized, in a softly ambiguous (expressively speaking) dialog between strings and woodwinds.

The next section might be called "supplication." It begins very hesitantly with quiet triplet figures in the violins culminating in yet another pathetic dying fall from flutes and clarinets. This introduces the most famous passage in the entire work, the haunting flute solo that has become the *locus classicus* for the expression of pathos in purely instrumental music. The music brightens over the next variation, a dialog in three-note fragments among the woodwinds gently accompanied by strings, leading to a calm chorale in broken phrases, first on the trombones, then with the entire wind section participating, *pianissimo*, as the music trails off into near silence.

With a shock, the passacaglia theme returns even more violently than at the beginning thanks to a fortissimo downward scale on the violins and violas (notice how the bass line's rising scale is continually opposed by the descending lines of so many of the variations). The next series of variations might be characterized as fear (shuddering strings over chattering winds), bravado (major-ish key, jagged leaping motives), and anxiety (scampering pianissimo strings in rapid triplet dialog with the woodwinds). As the anxiety grows the passacaglia theme sounds in the horns and returns to the fore once again, now blasted out by the full orchestra with violent, three-note jabs in the strings after each note.

The three-note jabs continue in the winds and timpani as the strings grind out a searing recapitulation of the initial woodwind theme. A semblance of calm returns abruptly and envelops the next few variations, as the woodwinds attempt to divert the music toward pastoral major keys, but the strings will hear nothing of it, and with a sudden forte outburst the music drives full bore with strongly marked rhythms into the coda. There's some wonderfully primal harmony here: the orchestra piles up a crescendo like rushing water pummeling a rapidly weakening dam.

This time, the dam bursts. Once again the passacaglia theme returns in close to its original fanfare form. Brahms marks it "faster"—a designation that few conductors honor to the degree that they should. Jochum (EMI) handles this passage particularly well. The orchestra now rises in fury—a last desperate effort to escape the confines of its omnipresent bass line. Bellicose trombones and despairing violins confront a series of crashing chords, the sound of a door slamming shut once and for all. With the tension at its highest point, Brahms gives himself over entirely to his rage, storming to the end with a flurry of strings and a last, defiant shout.

Although he would live for another dozen years after completing the Fourth, Brahms wrote no more symphonies. Indeed, he completed only one further orchestral work, the Double Concerto for Violin and Cello, a piece that has never equaled the popularity of his other symphonies or concertos. Perhaps he felt that with the Fourth he had done all that he could with the form, and if so it would be difficult to disagree. It's a work that captures Brahms' reverence for the Classical tradition, remains a true product of the Romantic age, and points the way forward to the twentieth century. In short, it represents a genuine summation, a microcosm of everything that the man stood for and believed in, as well as an unflinching dose of realism from one of the Romantic era's greatest and ultimately loneliest figures.

$\mathcal{D}$iscography of Recommended Recordings

GIVEN THE POPULARITY of his music, it should come as no surprise that the Brahms symphonies enjoy more recordings than just about any other pieces of classical music, rivaled only by Beethoven's symphonies. The proliferation of complete Brahms cycles, as opposed to individual performances, has been encouraged by the fact that (a) every conductor plays the music, (b) there are only four symphonies, making the entire proposition less expensive than a Beethoven cycle, and (c) the stylistic range from one work to the next isn't as wide as it is in, say, Beethoven, Haydn, Mahler, or even Tchaikovsky and Dvorák, tending (for good or ill) to yield more consistent results. Toss in the reality that just about any professional orchestra today knows the music practically by heart, and you would think that a new Brahms cycle stands a very good chance of being successful.

You would be wrong. There is more lousy Brahms out there than just about any other composer. By "lousy" I don't mean badly played in terms of getting the notes, but boring, rhythmically flabby, badly balanced, heavy, thick, and expressively inhibited. Even if you dispute the notion that

Brahms was not a particularly great orchestrator, it's incredibly easy to make him sound much worse than he really is. I have already pointed out that two conductors famous for their Brahms (Toscanini and Furtwängler) made a mess of the Third Symphony, but that's only the tip of a huge iceberg of musical mediocrity that spans almost a century of recorded music.

The roster of inconsistent, not very interesting, or even downright dismal Brahms cycles includes some very big names: George Szell (Sony), Leonard Bernstein (DG), Herbert von Karajan (DG), Karl Böhm (DG), Daniel Barenboim (Warner), Carlo Maria Giulini (DG), Bernard Haitink (Philips, twice), Riccardo Muti (Philips), Christoph Eschenbach (Virgin), Kurt Masur (Philips), Adrian Boult (EMI), John Barbirolli (EMI), Riccardo Chailly (Decca), and far too many others to waste space listing here.

Happily, there are also some exceptionally fine complete cycles as well as terrific individual performances (some of which comprise the best of the cycles just mentioned). Here, in no particular order, is a brief listing of the finest of them. Some performances have already been mentioned in the previous discussions, but it makes sense, for the sake of convenience, to summarize them all here.

Complete Cycles

Otto Klemperer/Phiharmonica Orchestra (EMI)

Christoph von Dohnanyí/Cleveland Orchestra (Warner/ Teldec)

Günter Wand/NDR Symphony Orchestra (RCA—his first cycle 1982/1983)

James Levine/Chicago Symphony or Vienna Philharmonic (RCA or DG)

Claudio Abbado/Berlin Philharmonic (DG)

Georg Solti/Chicago Symphony Orchestra (Decca)

Eugen Jochum/Berlin Philharmonic or London Philharmonic (DG or EMI)

Charles Mackerras/Scottish Chamber Orchestra (Telarc)

Eduard van Beinum/Concertgebouw Orchestra of Amsterdam (Philips)

Marek Janowski/Pittsburgh Symphony Orchestra (PentaTone)

Individual Symphonies

Symphony No. 1

Toscanini/Philharmonia Orchestra or NBC Symphony (Testament or RCA)

Wilhelm Furtwängler/NDR Symphony Orchestra (1951) (Tahra)

Carlo Maria Giulini/Los Angeles Philharmonic (DG)

Karl Böhm/Berlin Philharmonic (DG)

Symphony No. 2

Carlo Maria Giulini/Los Angeles Philharmonic (DG)

Pierre Monteux/Concertgebouw Orchestra of Amsterdam (Philips)

Bruno Walter/New York Philharmonic or Columbia Symphony Orchestra (Sony Classical)

Symphony No. 3

Bruno Walter/Columbia Symphony Orchestra (Sony Classical)

Marin Alsop/London Philharmonic (Naxos)

Carlo Maria Giulini/Vienna Philharmonic (DG)

Symphony No. 4

Carlos Kleiber/Vienna Philharmonic (DG)

Fritz Reiner/Royal Philharmonic (Chesky)

Leopold Stokowski/London Symphony Orchestra (RCA)

George Szell/Cleveland Orchestra (Sony Classical)

Annotated Bibliography

THE LITERATURE ON BRAHMS is understandably vast, and I make no attempt to summarize it here. Instead, I merely want to suggest a few places to continue your own explorations at your leisure. If you are interested in a good basic biography, Jan Swafford's *Johannes Brahms: A Biography* (Vintage, 1997) is pretty hard to beat, even if he does dwell a bit too much on the psychology of Brahms' questionable (according to the latest scholarship) childhood experiences playing the piano in flophouses on the Hamburg docks. As a corrective to this view, you can't do better than Styra Avins' *Johannes Brahms: Life and Letters* (Oxford University Press, 1997), which contains a very informative introductory essay as well as a very helpful narrative that puts the various letters in their proper context.

For those looking for a more thorough grounding in the technical workings of the symphonies than I can offer, Walter Frisch's *Brahms: The Four Symphonies* (Yale University Press, 1996) offers an excellent point of reference. Frisch also provides fascinating chapters on the state of the German symphony before Brahms appeared on the scene, and the performance history of the symphonies in the years following their premieres. Even if you can't follow all of the harmonic analysis, his book contains a mountain of useful and interesting information packed into a very reasonable length. Donald Francis Tovey's articles on the Brahms orchestral works (all of them) in his *Essays in Musical Analysis* (Oxford University Press, 1935) are also classics in their genre.

Finally, to get a flavor of the period and a fuller picture of Brahms and his circle from primary sources, you might want to try George Henschel's *Personal Recollections of Johannes Brahms* (Gorham Press, 1907), and *Letters from and to Joseph Joachim* (ed. Nora Bickley, Vienna House, 1972).